Key West City, Florida USA

Travel Guide

Author
Caleb Gray.

SONITTEC PUBLISHING. All rights reserved. No part of this publication may be reproduced, distributed, or transmitted in any form or by any means, including photocopying, recording, or other electronic or mechanical methods, without the prior written permission of the publisher, except in the case of brief quotations embodied in critical reviews and certain other noncommercial uses permitted by copyright law. For permission requests, write to the publisher, addressed "Attention: Permissions Coordinator," at the address below.

Copyright © 2019 Sonittec Publishing
All Rights Reserved

First Printed: 2019.

Publisher:
SONITTEC LTD
College House, 2nd Floor
17 King Edwards Road,
Ruislip
London
HA4 7AE

Table of Content

- **SUMMARY** 1
- **INTRODUCTION** 5
- **HISTORY OF KEY WEST** 11
  - THE ORIGIN 18
  - HERE COMES THE NAVY 20
  - LEGALIZING WRECKING 24
  - THE CIVIL WAR LOOMS 31
  - THE KEY WEST CIGAR 33
  - THE SPANISH AMERICAN WAR 38
  - THE IRON HORSE ARRIVES 42
  - LEAN TIMES 48
  - WORLD WAR II 51
  - PINK GOLD 56
- **KEY WEST TRAVEL AND TOURISM** 61
  - QUICK GUIDE 61
    - Climate 61
    - Getting in 62
    - Getting around 70
    - Seeing 72
    - Doing 75
    - Buying 85
    - Eating 87
    - Sleeping 97
    - Cope 112
    - Stay Safe 112
  - VACATION RENTAL AVAILABILITY 114
    - By The Beautiful Sea 114
    - Villa Nouveau Key West 120
    - Villa Deja vu Key West 125
    - Caribbean Cottage 135
    - Key West Wabi Sabi 141
    - A Tropical Tradition (Gallup Arms) 152
    - Lazy Iguana 156
  - SUMMERTIME THINGS TO DO (ON THE WATER) 161
  - THINGS TO DO, IN KEY WEST 171
    - Cultural Sights 181
    - Food and Drink 192

- Casual Dining 195
  - Mellow Cafe and Gastropub 195
  - AZUR 197
  - Duetto Pizza & Gelato 198
  - OnlyWood 199
  - Thirsty Mermaid 201
  - The Salty Angler 202
  - Sandy's Cafe 203
  - Date and Thyme (formerly Help Yourself) 205
  - Mangoes 206
- Coffee Shops 207
- 5 Brothers Grocery & Sandwich Shop 208
- Shopping 246
- Key West Wedding Information 266
- Activities 268
  - Dolphin Encounters 268
  - Dry Tortugas 269
  - Fishing 271
  - Glassbottom Boats 272
  - Golf 273
  - Kayak Tours 276
  - Sunset Sails 277
  - Sunset at Mallory Square 278
  - African Cemetery at Higgs Beach 280
  - Audubon House & Garden 281
- Museum 283
  - Firehouse Museum 283
  - Flagler Station & Overseas Railway Historium 287
  - Custom's House 288
  - Shipwreck Museum 289
  - Florida Keys Eco-Discovery Center 290
  - Mel Fisher Maritime Museum 292
  - Oldest House Museum & Garden 293
  - Turtle Kraals Museum 293
  - Hemingway House 295
  - Truman's Little White House 296
  - Key West Lighthouse & Keeper's Museum 297
  - East Martello 298
  - Audubon House & Garden 299

Summary

The importance of travelling in our life?

Everyone has their very own reasons to travel. Some people travel for work, some travel for pleasure while for others it is just a way of life. They travel to live and to escape at the same time.

Whatever might be the reason to travel, here are few ways in which travelling would definitely change you and I think that is why travelling becomes so important in life:

<u>Enjoy being alone</u>: There is something therapeutic about being alone and being at peace with it. While you soak in a new culture, you also connect with your own inner self.

<u>Learn to adapt</u>: It is a different world out there, literally. Be it the pace of life, the language or simply the change in weather, it is always a change and you have to adapt to it. This is what makes travelling truly beautiful as you break away from the routine and adapt to something totally new.

<u>Experience a new culture</u>: Every place comes with its distinct cultural habits, you cannot think about New York without talking about its fast paced life and about Italy without enjoying its relaxed lifestyle. Similarly, while visiting the UK you might have to be a bit formal in your interactions with the locals, on the other hand, while greeting the people in Thailand, one can be really warm and casual.

<u>Broaden your taste buds</u>: Travelling without experiencing the local food is just not complete. It is not only a culinary experience but a cultural one as well.

Key West City, Florida USA

<u>Get out of comfort zone</u>: From simple experiences like the weather, way of life or food to the more adventurous ones like trying a new sport, travelling really pushes ones boundaries to the core. You might end up participating in a street carnival in Brazil just like the locals or trying the local delicacies (read insects) in Thailand.

<u>Indulge in Photography</u>: It does not matter whether you are a professional or not. It is also irrelevant whether you have a DSLR or a very basic camera, while travelling what matters is the love and quest for seeing beautiful places and the sheer joy of capturing them in your lense. Travelling would in return give you your very own collection of amazing postcards of beautiful sunsets, snow laced mountains or sunny beaches.

<u>Learn to escape</u>: Travelling is the best way to break the routine. If you are in a bustling city, go ahead and experience the country life. If you are in a rural place, travel to a bustling city and experience its madness.

Stressed with the city life or work pressure? A spa break in Himalayas or Kerala is a must try.

Appreciate Nature: The quest to explore more when one is travelling always leads to a sense of amazement about nature. While most of us keep a track of technological advancements, Nature has its own ways of outshining all of these. The Antelope Canyon in Arizona or Turquoise Ice in Russia are the finest examples of this. For more, check out the most unbelievable places around the world.

Get closer to your own roots: While one travels and experiences a lot of different cultures and practices, it definitely brings one closer to his or her own roots. Travel helps one appreciate one's identity and culture.

Travelling is all about experiences. They can happen in terms of culture, people, places but most importantly with one's own self and this was all about

Introduction

Key West is the southern most city in the United States. It sits on the last major island at the end of the Florida Keys. The weather ranges from balmy, hot, & humid to quite pleasant in the winter months. The rainy season is in the summer time.

The dry season is during the winter months. Temperatures in Key West during the middle of January often are in the low 80's when the rest of the nation is being blanketed by snow drifts or is fighting floods. As a result, the winter and Spring months are a great time to visit and there are plenty of hotels in Key West to choose from. The humidity tends to be the lowest during the winter months.

During the summer months the humidity is quite high; the temperatures hover around the high 80's or low 90's and rain showers are common. The hurricane season officially begins in July, but most of the dangerous hurricanes arrive in August and September.

Key West was discovered by Ponce de Leon on May 13, 1513. In later years Key West became home to many pirates. As recently as the seventies and early 80's smugglers were using Key West to unload their drugs. Key West was once the richest city in Florida, in the late 1880's. "Wrecking" used to be a profitable job in Key West in the early 1800's. This involved salvaging treasure from many of the sunken vessels that litter the bottom of the local waters. Cigar factories were extremely profitable in the late 1880's and Key West was the cigar capital of the world. As with the other Keys, Key West is built on an old coral reef. This means the soil quality is rather poor. Most people in the Keys have to pay high prices for water because it is taken directly from the ocean and then desalinated.

For the most part the Keys do not have their own aquifers and water needs to be taken from the ocean. Unlike the rest of the United States the price for water is higher than the price for electricity.

Highway One which is the only road leading to and out of Key West is an interesting and enjoyable ride. It is marked with mile markers, mile 110 is near Key Largo and mile marker 0 is in Key West at the corner of Fleming and Whitehead Streets. US 1 traverses about 110 miles of islands known as the Florida Keys. Each island is unique in appearance however; all have their share of mangrove trees, coconut palm trees, and tropical beachside bars. A very impressive part of the roadway is the seven-mile bridge.

As you enter this bridge you have the feeling that you somehow are driving into the ocean. All you can see ahead of you is miles of water. Next to the seven-mile bridge is the old 7-mile bridge. Parts of it are now missing and it shows its age. Key West has been the home to many famous writers and artists. Some names that come to mind are Ernest Hemmingway, Tennessee Williams, Robert Frost, and Jimmy Buffet. Key West is a centrally located bustling port town. Coming to Key West to write or otherwise? Why not stay in luxury try the <u>Parrot Key Resort and Spa</u>

It has a tropical Caribbean flavor to it, especially with the inter mixing of various island cultures. There are also many, many tropical plants that grow here. In fact Southern Florida is a haven for tropical fruit and vegetation. Many of the species grown here, cannot grow in the rest of the United States. Besides some of the really rare plant and tree species, expect to see many coconut palms, hibiscus, and bougainvillea. Watch out for the coconut palms. They may leave you with "Coconut Amnesia" as Lenore Troia sings about in her album Jetset to Sunset. The Famous Point in Key West.

For more information about Lenore and her excellent lively island music, please visit her site at: www.lenoretroia.com Click on her "sounds" link on the left side of the webpage and you will soon be hopping along to the tunes! Some of my favorites are off of the <u>Jetset to Sunset</u> album among them, Jetset to Sunset, Coconut Amnesia, & Save Me From The Real World. Sometimes memories are made with music and I hold good memories of driving in The Keys listening to Lenore's music full blast with the windows down!

Duval Street is the heart of Key West running for approximately a mile from water to water (Atlantic Ocean to the Gulf of Mexico). There are many unique shops (to be listed and described in detail later), restaurants, and clubs located here. Hemingway, Frost, and more recently, Buffet (a God in the Florida Keys), used to call some of these clubs their personal watering holes. At night this street becomes alive with young people drinking and dancing and partying hard. Concert halls, clubs, piano bars, and pubs each contribute their own flavor to the ambiance of this street on a warm tropical evening.

As you walk around town notice the unique architecture of the local buildings. Key West has one of the largest historical districts in the United States with over 3000 structures on the National Register of Historical Places. The homes range from modest to elaborate Victorian mansions.

The largest of the early homes were built by sea captains. Prices for lodging and food tend to be a bit expensive in Key West. This is in part because of the limited space on the island.

History of Key West

Climate
Frost free zone

Key West claims to be the only city in the lower 48 states never to have had a frost. Due to the proximity of the Gulf Stream in the Straits of Florida, about 12 miles (19 km) south and southeast, and the softening effects of the Gulf of Mexico to the west and north, Key West has a notably mild, tropical climate,(Koppen climate classification Aw, similar to the Caribbean islands), where the average temperatures during winter are about 14 degrees (lower than in summer). Cold fronts are heavily modified by the warm tropical water as they move in from northerly quadrants in winter. The average low and high temperatures in

January are 67 °F/ 75 °F. There is no known record of frost, ice, sleet, or snow in Key West. The coldest temperature ever recorded in Key West was 41 °F (5 °C) on January 12, 1886, and on January 13, 1981. Prevailing easterly tradewinds and sea breezes suppress the usual summertime heating. The average low and high temperatures in July are 81 °F/ 90 °F. The hottest temperature ever recorded in Key West was 97 °F (36.1 °C) on July 19, 1880, and on August 26, 1956.

Rainy and dry seasons
Precipitation is characterized by dry and wet seasons. The time of November through April receives abundant sunshine and slightly less than 25 percent of the annual rainfall. This rainfall usually happens in advance of cold fronts in a few light or heavy showers. May through October is normally the wet season, receiving approximately 53 percent of the yearly total in numerous tropical showers and thunderstorms. Rain falls on most days during the wet season. Early morning is the popular time for these showers, which

is different from mainland Florida, where showers and thunderstorms usually occur in the late afternoon. Easterly (tropical) waves during this season occasionally bring excessive rainfall, while infrequent hurricanes may be accompanied by unusually heavy amounts. At any rate, Key West is the driest city in Florida.

Hurricanes

Hurricanes rarely hit Key West and the little island has been relatively lucky. Locals say that Hurricane Wilma on October 24, 2005, was the worst storm in recent memory. The entire island was told to evacuate and business owners were forced to close their shops. After the hurricane had passed, a storm surge sent 8' of sea water inland, completely inundating a large portion of the lower Keys. Low-lying areas of Key West and the lower Keys, including major tourist destinations were under up to 3' of water. Sixty percent of the homes in Key West were flooded. The higher parts of Old Town, such as the Solares Hill and cemetery areas, did not flood due to their higher elevations of 12-18'. The surge destroyed tens of thousands of cars throughout the lower Keys, and many houses were flooded with 1-2 feet of sea water. A local newspaper referred to Key West and the lower Keys as a "car graveyard." The peak of the storm surge occurred when the eye of Wilma had already passed over the Naples, area, and the sustained winds during the surge were less than 40 mph (64 km/h). The storm destroyed the piers at the clothing optional Atlantic Shores Motel and breached the shark tank at the Key West Aquarium, freeing its sharks. Damage postponed the island's famous Halloween Fantasy Fest until the following December. MTV's The Real World: Key West was filming during the hurricane and deals with the storm.

In March 2006, the NOAA opened its National Weather Forecasting building on White Street. The building is designed to withstand a Category 5 hurricane and its storm surge.

The most intense previous hurricane was Hurricane Georges, a Category 2, in September 1998. The storm damaged many of the houseboats along Houseboat Row in the Cow Key channel on the northwest corner.

The History
Key West, like the other Florida Keys, began as a coral forest under the sea water - marine life was its population. As the polar ice caps reformed and the sea level dropped, terrestrial plant and animal life found its way. Soil was formed by decaying organic matter and storm actions. For millenniums the ocean continued to drop and the ocean currents, wind currents, birds, etc. continued to propagate the islands. Eventually human life forms found their way. This pyramiding of trillions of life cells, along with the forces of nature, produced an island called Cayo Hueso by early Spanish travelers.

A note on the word "Key" used to identify an island. Its origin is not well established except by usage. Most believe that it began by the Spanish adapting the word "cayo' from the Taino Indians of Hispanola and Cuba referring to small islands. The Spanish normally used "isla" for island and "islet" for small island. At least in the New World, they appear to use "cayo" and "cayuelo" for a very small island. The English used "Cay" or "Kay" such as Cay Sal Banks. Cay is pronounced by Americans as the letter "K," but by Englishmen as the word 'Key.' I am not certain if the written and the pronounced versions made any difference. Anyway, English maps of the Keys made just prior to the Revolutionary War of 1776 used the word "Key." A Colonial American court record of the "Libel of Dennis and Allen vs the snow St. Fermin alias Britanis" in 1744 used the word "Keys" referring to the Florida Keys. This is one case where an American court reporter might write ''Key' when an Englishmen prounced 'Cay.' See the Admiralty Papers, Vol. 2, 1743 - 1744.

The native aborigines and subsequent native groups were the first settlers of Key West. The Europeans were tourists for its first 300 odd years of historic existence. Europeans stopped for fresh water on these islands, which stood as silent as the martyrs for which they were first named. The silence was broken occasionally by those seeking refuge from being shipwrecked, to fish, to lumber, to salvage, etc. Other than the Native Americans, apparently no one settled permanently until about the time Florida became a United States territory in 1821. There are scattered references, but no specifics, to New Englanders and Bahamians as permanent settlers before the early 1800s.

The history of Key West is much like the rest of the Keys until 1821. Its natural deep water port was the deepest port between New Orleans and Norfolk, Virginia. Key West quickly became an economic center, was settled rapidly and became Florida's largest populated city. It had professional residents such as doctors, lawyers, insurance representatives, politicians, military personnel, journalists, publishers, etc. most of whom by vocation made some written documentation.

These documentation's have made Key West history easier to be 'history', not fable. Politically, Key West was Monroe County. In population alone it overwhelmed all the remaining Keys for about a century and a half. Therefore, the following is nowhere a complete outline of its history.

The Origin

From a historian's point of view, Key West has an interesting beginning. To be considered is the island's ownership as private property, ownership by the Territory of Florida, ownership by the U.S. Government and finally as a local incorporated entity. John W. Simonton purchased the island on January 19, 1822 from Juan Pablo Salas, who had acquired it as a Spanish Land Grant in 1815 from Don Juan de Estrata, but as a new U.S. Territory the original Don Juan de Estrata Land Grant to Salas had to the confirmed - no U.S. deed could be granted. In reality it went round and round with claims and counter claims.

Attempts to follow these look like a spider web. John Simonton soon took on three northern partners: John Whitehead, John Fleeming and Pardon Greene. On the scene arrived General John Geddes of Charleston who had also purchased Key West. It was discovered that Don Juan Salas had sold it twice, first to John Strong, a lawyer no less, and then to Simonton. As if this were not bad enough, Strong had also previously sold Key West to George Murray before John Geddes. In summary, Salas sold it twice, Strong and Simonton, and Strong twice, Murray and Geddes. Simonton had already divided it up amongst three others: Whitehead, Fleeming and Greene. Greene made several strategic moves by buying up claims in his name.

On May 23, 1828, Congress acknowledged the land grant of Salas was confirmed. Simonton as the legal owner. We might surmise that this was Florida's first land scam. Amazing as it legally appears, the Territory of Florida with an Act of Incorporation incorporated the City of Key West on January 8, 1828. I have never fully researched this, but my understanding with Monroe County's Territorial Representative Richard Fitzpatrick changed its name to the Town of Key West on November 28, 1828. This was probably repealed? Fitzpatrick was the one who made Indian Key the County Seat of Dade County.

Here Comes the Navy

When England possessed Florida in 1763, the Spanish contended that the Keys was North Havana. On March 25, 1822, Navy Lt. Commandant Matthew C. Perry sailed the Navy schooner *Shark* to Key West, surveyed and planted the U.S. flag, physically claiming the Keys as United States property. There were no protests so the Keys were United States property. The same year the president authorized a custom house at Key West. Mr. Joel Yancy was the first collector of customs.

For history purposes, Lt. Perry did cause a minor confusion. He renamed Cayo Hueso (Key West) to

"Thompson's Island" for the Secretary of the Navy Smith Thompson and the harbor "Port Rogers" for the president of the Board of Navy Commissioners.

As to the name Key West, there is little doubt that it was some form of translation from the Spanish 'Cayo' (Key) and 'Hueso', if indeed the name was Hueso. The Spanish word Hueso (Way-so) means bone in English. A few believe that it came from the seven-year apple tree found in the Keys, which was also called hueso by the Spanish. Regardless of its origin, the name Key West prevailed with time.

Piracy was a problem in the West Indies open waters and Congress decided to protect US shipping. The task was given to the Navy. Partly on reports by Lt. Perry, the Navy on February 1, 1823, ordered Commodore David Porter to establish a depot in Key West to end piracy. Slave ships were included as an act of piracy.

The aforementioned civilians preceded the military into Key West. However, they were having problems deciding who was the rightful owner. Commodore David Porter arrived in April 1823 with his West Indies Squadron to establish the depot.

Commodore Porter had no problem knowing who owned Thompson's Island, the United States did, and he simply took charge. He supported the name of Thompson's Island and Port Rogers; and further named the naval depot 'Allenton' after Lt. William Allen who was killed by pirates. For some it was difficult to determine who disliked Commodore Porter more, the pirates or the residents of 'Thompson's Island.' It should be noted that the civilian residents knew that their success totally depended on the military defending the island. Porter lost his command in 1825 and in 1826 the Navy moved the Navy base to Pensacola. A coal and supply facility remained at Key West.

In October 1824 one of Porter's officers heard stolen goods were stored in Fajardo, Puerto Rico. When he landed without permission, he was seized, imprisoned as a pirate and later released. Enraged, Porter marched ashore with 200 men and compelled the Spanish to make atonement for their actions. It is a long story but it was deemed that he exceeded his authority and was suspended by court-martial. In August 1826 he resigned and became the General of Marine for Mexico's navy. In this capacity he also haunted the residents of Key West in the years to come.

However, Commodore Porter was extremely successful in protecting Key West from pirates, but he could not protect it from yellow fever, lack of fresh water and the 'wrecking' industry. (See the General History page on wrecking.) Key West was a 'natural' for the relatively new US industry of salvaging wrecked ships. It had a natural deep water seaport, was situated on the primary shipping route and had a natural resource in its front yard - the Florida Reefs. The Gulf Stream route was irresistible as a shipping route and in many cases practically unavoidable. Some of the richest cargoes passed and wrecked in its front yard. All they had to do was sit back and wait.

Legalizing Wrecking

Location, location, location is the cry of any good businessman. Then, in 1825 the Federal Wrecking Act prescribed that all property wrecked in US waters be taken to a US Port of Entry. Commodore Porter left the same year for Pensacola. 1828 was a pivotal year. In 1828 Key West was designated a Port of Entry. Key West grew from a desolated island into a bustling city within a few years. Congress acknowledged Simonton as the owner and Key West incorporated twice, once as a city on January 8, 1928, then as a town on Novmber 28, 1928. Congress created the 'Superior Court of the Southern District' with admiralty power. Judge James Webb was its first judge, but his successor, William Marvin, will be the most remembered. He authored the Law of Wreck and Salvage and later was provisional governor of Florida at the close of the Civil War. In 1832, Key West reverted to a charter type city government.

During this time John Whitehead's brother, William, surveyed the city in 1829. Southard was the Secretary of the Navy, hence Southard Street and Eaton was Secretary of the Army, hence Eaton Street. William Duval was the first Territorial Governor of Florida, hence Duval Street.

Wrecking could provide quick monetary rewards. One of the early Charleston settlers in Key West was Richard Fitzpatrick. Fitzpatrick was 30-years old when he arrived in Key West. He became the only authorized auctioneer for wrecking property before the 1828 law. Reportedly in one year he made around $10,000 in fees alone. This would be equivalent to about $280,000 today. We will read of his name later.

Two years after the aforementioned 1828 events, the census of 1830 revealed Key West's population was 517. The year before, 258 acres were mapped as a town with 64 blocks. These early settlers were primarily from the New England states, not the Bahamas. Key West grew as a maritime, a military and a county seat community. By 1850 there were 2,645 and in 1890 there were 18,080 residents.

Key West had its first newspaper, the *Register,* in 1829. The *Key West Gazette* followed in 1831, then the *Enquirer* in 1834. The present day *Key West Citizen* began as *The Citizen* in 1904 and consolidated with *The Inter-Ocean*.

Around 1830, salt production began in the present day airport's general area. There was a large need for salt for food preservation. About 50,000 bushels of salt was usual, however an early rainy season could 'wash' away the profits. William Whitehead and Richard Fitzpatrick were prominent salt producers. Wrecking remained the economy of Key West of which Fitzpatrick owned several wrecking ships. The military history continued with the arrival of the US Army in 1831. Major James Glassel commanded two companies camped on North

Beach. This was good timing as the Second Seminole War was approaching. The Army was to be a larger influence that originally expected.

Wrecking however was the real industry of the Keys. A sad but curious wreck occurred in 1831. In December, the ship *Maria* wrecked on the reef and the wreckers save all of its 250 passengers and crew. They were brought to Key West which according to the 1830 census had a total population of only 517. Somehow, the residents took care of all the survivors until arrangements could be made.

Jacob Housman, also a wrecker, did not get along well with the Key West wrecking courts, so he sought to establish a port of entry on Indian Key. He did not succeed; however, he upset the tranquility, such as it was, of Monroe County. He was not alone in this feat as by now Richard Fitzpatrick had been elected several times to Florida's Legislative Council. Housman and 56 others had petitioned for the division of Monroe

County. One of the main stated objections was traveling to Key West for jury duty.

One reason for presenting this history is our current tendency of thinking of Monroe County only as it exists today. Fitzpatrick had become Monroe County's Territorial Council Representative at Tallahassee. In 1836 he was elected the council president and easily pushed through a bill dividing Monroe County. This established the entire eastern section of former Monroe County as Dade County on February 4, 1836. The size of Monroe County was reduced by about half with Key West as its major settlement. Fitzpatrick had since the 1830s acquired extensive land holdings in the new county of Dade. Indian Key was the county seat.

In December 1835 the Second Seminole War commenced with the killing of Major Francis Dade. (See web page on the Seminoles.) Throughout the entire Florida War, Key West was never attacked. However, on August 7, 1840, Indian Key was attacked and burned except for one house. (See web page on Indian Key.)

One of the outcomes of the War of 1812 was a coastal defense system. Extensive plans followed developing usually brick fortifications. Construction of Fort Taylor by the US Army began in 1845 only to experience major destruction the next year by the Hurricane of 1846. Work continued on the brick structure in time to be a major influence at the outbreak of the Civil War. Another 1845 brick structure was the completion of the two-story Marine Hospital on August 2, 1845. Originally built for the U.S. Merchant Marine the 40-bed hospital served many until its closure in February 1943.

A new industry was looming for Key West - the sponge industry. The value of processed sponges was realized in the 1840s. The Bahamians were well adapted for this occupation and came to Key West in droves. Key West quickly became a sponge center and this industry helped Key West when the wrecking industry slowed down. It was also an alternate job while the wreckers were awaiting a wreck to occur. As the 1850 census records indicate, Key West rebuilt after the destruction of the 1846 hurricane. The construction of Fort Taylor, the sponge industry and the highly successful wrecking industry contributed to Keys West's rapid growth. Key West began to lose the sponge monopoly to Florida's west coast around 1870.

Some experts estimate that if today's measuring devices had been available, the Great Hurricane of 1846 (October 11 and 12) would have been a category-5 hurricane. The collector of customs, Steven Mallory, wrote that of 600 houses all but eight were destroyed or damaged. The offshore Sand Key and harbor lighthouses were destroyed. Water rose to about 8-feet in the lower streets. Did this discourage the residents? Evidently not as the above enumeration's indicate about a 300 percent growth between 1840 and 1850. In May 1859 Key West experienced the first of its large fires. A fire in the L.M. Shaefer warehouse burned all but two houses in the two blocks formed by Green, Front, Simonton and Whitehead streets. -

The Civil War Looms

The work at Fort Taylor was the first federal permanent building in Key West since Commodore Porter. At the outset of the Civil War, Florida was a confederate state. It was expected that Key West would be also. The Union had a considerable force in Key West because of the construction of Fort Taylor under Captain E. B. Hunt (Corps of Engineers). Key West was taken easily when at night on January 13, 1861, Captain James Brannan took possession of the city while it slept. Key West played a major role during the war because of it strategic location. A special city election was conducted to replace all the previously elected officers. Alexander Patterson was elected mayor.

The Civil War was largely responsible for Key West becoming Florida's largest city. Competing cities in size were to the north and some, as Jacksonville, suffered considerably. Key West was the center of the Union's Gulf and East Gulf blockading forces and profited economically. Many ships from many nations were seized and brought into Key West's harbor for disposition. Work finally began on the two Martello Towers. Key West also was the support base for Fort Jefferson. How the city government of Key West functioned is not clear.

On December 8, 1866, Monroe County got part of its original land back when its present boundary was established starting "at the mouth of Broad Creek, a stream separating Cayo Largo from Old Roads [sic] Key, extending thence in a direct line to Mudd Point." This places the north boundary at about Mile Marker 114.

Shipping lanes connected Key West with the world, but in 1866 another step was taken. Key West became the hub for the International Ocean Telegraph Company (IOTC) underwater cable line. The line connected Havana, Cuba to Punta Rassa on Monroe County's west coast to the United States. On August 21, 1867 the mayor of Key West exchanged telegrams with Cuban Captain-General Joaquin Manzanos. It paid a huge role for the United States to have communications with Cuba in the Spanish American War (1898). The Key West cable manager, Martin Hellings, operated an intelligence office for the U.S. government.

After a half century of settling, the 1870 census shows Key West's population as 5,675. In the same half century the total Upper Keys for five islands population was 133. No one lived on Lower Matecumbe Key, the sixth principal island.

The Key West Cigar

One should not overlook the influence of the Cuban population. They had continually grown since William Wall, an Englishman, started a Key West cigar factory in 1831. The Cuban Independence War of 1868 (Ten Years War) assured Key West of becoming a cigar capital. Spanish became the second language. The *El*

Republicano newspaper was printed in Spanish is 1870. It went farther than this; in 1875 Carlos Cespedes was elected mayor. The economic timing of this new force was great as lighthouses were being built and the wrecking industry was destined to decline. The coming of the steam ship also greatly reduced the number of ships that wrecked.

Cuban cigar workers were accustomed to unions, but they were weak at first. As labor union membership grew, their power grew. In 1885 there was a major cigar worker's strike which lasted for months and Vicente Ybor, a principal manufacturer, moved to Tampa. Of course, Tampa offered a variety of 'good deals' and other cigar companies or individual workers followed.

Fire was no stranger in Key West and Key Westers were always vigilant for fire in their mostly wooded city. Recorded in 1843 was the burning of a waterfront warehouse. The simple fire fighting equipment proved almost useless and was thrown into the water in disgust. Again in 1859 the city was tested by flames which took out a small section. One person intentionally blew up his house to make a fire gap. Then in 1886 a fire destroyed the entire downtown section in the early morning hours of April 1. This was not April fools. The fire started at 2 a.m. in the San Carlos Hall on Duval Street between Fleming and Southard streets. High winds fanned the flames while an inadequate fire fighting system fought almost in vain - the primary steam operated fire engine was in New York for repairs. Again, blowing up buildings was done, but three people died in the process. Twelve hours later over 50 buildings, one the cigar box manufacturer, and six wharves were destroyed. Four lost their lives. When one sees a historic red brick building in Key West, most likely it was constructed after 1886.

One example was the red brick Key West Customs House at the end of Whitehead Street which has been wonderfully restored today. The contract for its construction was let in December 1888 and was occupied three years later. Its total cost was $107,955.96.

- Public Transportation -

The cigar industry also led Key West into the twentieth century in transportation. Eduardo Hidalgo Gato introduced a mule powered streetcar system to connect "Gatoville" to the downtown area in the 1880s. I am not certain of the exact date. Signs on the streetcars exhibited in early photos denotes it as the "K-W St Car Association."

The cigar industry was fraught with strikes. It was during one, or the threat of one, that Gato was more or less forces to sell mule driven system during a boycott of the line in 1894. A Cincinnati company purchased it and converted it to electric streetcars. The name Stone and Webster comes to my mind. The electric streetcars were removed from service in 1927 and the tracks removed.

You Can't Beat Success

By this time Key West was the largest city in Florida. To make it even larger in May 1889 the Florida Legislature granted a new charter to the city placing the entire island within the city limits. This change also provide power to float bonds for street improvements. Another charter change in 1891 authorized a mayor and made the city clerk, marshall, tax collector and assessor, treasurer and chief-of-police elected offices. Jacksonville eventually exceeded the population of Key West by incorporating most of Duval County - a numbers game. Successful cities spring back from almost overwhelming odds. Within a few years after the fire, Key West appeared to be better than ever. Mule drawn street cars appeared and the Peninsular and Occidental Steamship Company (P&O) began biweekly sailing's between Tampa, Key West and Havana. An electric power plant was operational as were, a new courthouse, a turtle canning plant, a new post office. They had to be new as they had been destroyed or damaged so badly that replacement was the only answer. In 1889 the Florida Legislature granted Key West a new charter expanding the city's boundaries to include the entire island. Partly due to the city limit boundary change, the population almost doubled between 1880 (9,890) and 1890 (18,080).

In the 1890s, the sponge market thrived. One entrepreneur was A. J. Arapian, a Greek immigrant known locally as the 'sponge king.' His annual sales approached $500,000.

The Spanish American War

In December of 1891 Jose Marti arrived from Tampa in Key West for his first visit to continue the work he had started in New York - organizing a Cuban revolution in earnest. He also visited and worked until he had the expatriated Cubans from all parts taking an active role. On February 25, 1895, the "Liberator of Cuba" gave the word for the revolution to start. Marti himself went to

Cuba and was killed in the battle of Dos Rios in May 1895.

Attempts were made to draw America into the confrontation. U.S. owned participants such as the ships *Three Friends* and *Dauntless* participated as filibusters. In an attempt to avoid neutrality laws, arms were taken on one ship and troops on another taking different routes. Covert actions became overt when The USS *Maine* left Key West, met with the Atlantic Fleet on training maneuvers in the Tortugas, and sailed into Havana Harbor on a peaceful mission. After 21 days at anchor, on February 15, 1898 at 9:40 P.M. she exploded sinking with a crew of 355. Only 94 survived. Key West citizens dedicated a monument in the city cemetery on March 15, 1900 to the heroes who died in the harbor of Havana on that February 15, 1898.

"Remember the Maine" became the rallying cry and Spanish - U.S. negotiations were in motion. Formal fighting began on April 22, 1898 and ended August 12, 1898. Key West became a focus of activities and drinking the supply of drinking water became a problem. A lemon aid was 20 cents and a beer 25 cents. Tampa was the primary support city but Key West was the center of activity. The U.S. Navy at Key West was again beefed up and played a significant role during the Spanish American War. After the war ended the navy facilities were downsized again. Years of Cuban revolutionary activity was over. Key West returned to some degree of normalcy but she began to loose some of the sponge market to Tarpon Springs.

Nearing the close of the 19th century, Key West found its primary economic force of wrecking dwindling. Almost 10,000 Cubans had made Key West their home which was almost half of its population. The cigar industry dominated Key West. An example was Pohalski village which was almost a town in itself including the cigar manufacturing buildings. Its center would be today in the area of White Street and Truman Avenue. (The Germans did much of the art work for the cigar labels.) Cigar making would continue to dominate

Key West until the 1920s when cigarette use brought it to its knees. After the Great Fire, public buildings were mostly of brick construction. Many of those constructed of wood added tin roofs to protect from blowing sparks from other houses on fire. This practice continues. Examples of brick structures are the US Customs House (1891), the Old City Hall (1891) and Old Monroe County Courthouse (1890).

The military continued in Key West as the US took more of an active interest in the Caribbean. Winter training was conducted in the Caribbean area and in 1906 a wireless communication system was started. Key West was a major center and continued to grow. The Key West Electric Street Railway Company operated its first street car on Duval Street on February 13, 1899. It transported nearly 500 passengers its first day. The same year the county constructed a road through the eastern portion of Key West - now Flagler Avenue.

The Iron Horse Arrives

Henry Morrison Flagler gave Key West its next shot in the arm. In 1905 men and material began spanning the Keys for a railroad to Key West. With this expectation, a new Chamber of Commerce met and elected W.D. Cash as president. Since land was scarce in Key West, Flagler dredged in new land for his railroad yard and docks. He thought on a large scale and had 1,700 foot docks for ocean liners plus for his future train ferries to Cuba. Miami was the headquarters for construction, but its destination with the huge land and sea terminal was Key West.

When Flagler was told there was not enough land for his massive rail terminal, he instructed his work force the "build some." Key West was enlarged with 134 acres of land fill pumped up the bottoms of the Gulf now called Trumbo. Trumbo was the dredging contractor. During the railroad construction period, Key West and the other Keys experienced three hurricanes - 1906, 1909 and 1910. As a result of building the railroad, Key West and Stock Island was connected the first time by a road in February 1906. The October 1909 hurricane did considerable damage to downtown Key West. In May 12, 1910 the first spike was driven for the railroad from the Key West end and the first train arrived with pomp and ceremony on January 22, 1912. (The railroad is covered on a separate web page.

Mr. Flagler died in 1913 and the Florida East Coast Railway was just getting its operation going when WW-I brought in more military to Key West again. On July 13, 1917, ground was broken for a coastal air patrol station on land rented from the F.E.C. Rwy. On September 22 the first naval flight was logged in - A Curtis N-9 seaplane piloted by Lt. Stanley Parker. Seaplane training and 'lighter-than-air' craft facilities were constructed for submarine patrol. On December 18, 1917, the Naval Air Base Key West was commissioned with Lt. Parker as its commanding officer. Naval Air Facility planes flew from rented land of the railroad yard at Trumbo Point. On January 8, 1918, the first flight of naval flight students arrived for seaplane training. The downtown Naval Station was expanded for destroyers and submarines. This marked the beginning of Key West as a naval training facility. The submarine base was not completed until 1932. Key West was abuzz with military once again. Much of the activity subsided when the war ended.

The Florida Land Boom during the 1920s brought increased tourist activity to Key West. One new addition was the F.E.C. Casa Marina hotel. In February 1918, the F.E.C. Railway purchased the property for $1,000. Construction began in the spring and the formal opening was New Years Eve, December 31, 1921. Louis Schutt was moved from the Long Key Fishing Camp to be the manager. It closed indefinitely in the spring of 1932 - the Great Depression had arrived in Key West. Afterwards it opened for a few months each winter until leased to support the US Navy in World War-II. John Spottswood purchased the

Casa Marina in June 1966 to begin operation by others than the F.E.C. The hotel was completely renovated in 1978.

While construction for the Casa Marina had just gotten underway, Key West experienced the severe Hurricane of 1919 on September 9. More than $2 million of damages were incurred by the category 4 hurricane.

Through out Florida a land boom was just awakening and land sales and building flourished. The Keys had a lot of vacant land but was available only by the railroad. The need for a vehicular highway was seen and in 1923 Monroe County approved $300,000 as a beginning. Also in 1923, Key West experienced another severe fire destroying about 43 houses in the White Street area. The estimate was $125,000 of damage and 40 families homeless.

In 1924 the La Concha hotel was created on Duval Street. After the 1926 hurricane more funds were needed for the highway so an additional $2,500,000 was approved. This would include three ferry boats to span a 40-mile open water space. The stock market crash of 1929 delivered the final blow to the 'Boom', but for south Florida the hurricane of 1926 signaled the end. Miami was the hub to support new development, was devastated by the hurricane and could not support the building process.

In July of 1926, Key West replaced its aging electric street cars with buses. The Overseas Highway was completed and officially opened in 1928 for two-way traffic to and from Key West via three ferry boats serving about 40 miles of the trip. In May 1929 the overland bus company, Florida Motor Lines began an extensive campaign to promote Key West as the tourist Mecca of Florida. Signs that Key West was really moving into the twentieth century was dozed in 1929 when Miss Lena Johnson, was the first woman to be elected to its city commission, was defeated for reelection, but it was only by 40 votes.

More transportation news was made in Key West at this time. In June 1927 the highway from Big Pine Key to Key West was opened. On October 28, 1927, Pan American Airline (PAA) pilots Huey Wells and Eddie Musick delivered 772 pounds of air-mail from Key West to Havana in a Fokker trimotor. The dream of pioneer Juan Terry Trippe and his airline Pan American was in operation and it began in Key West. Trippe was born in Seabright, N. J. in 1899, graduated Yale University after serving in the Naval Air Service in WW I and joined a firm of investment bankers. With his financial support of those such as the Whitneys, Vanderbuilts and Rockefellows, he gained the Key West to Havana U.S. mail contract on June 16, 1927 for PAA and the rest is history. Monroe County entered into the air transportation mode when it purchased the Key West International Airport in November 1952. The Navy made its last flight of an airship and all blimps were moved out in March 1959. In April 1968, National Air Lines made its first landing on extended runways using a Boeing 727.

Lean Times

The 1930s brought The Great Depression which had severe effects on Key West. The tourists and associated building of the 1920s evaporated. This was followed by the Navy reducing its base to maintenance status in 1932 (the Navy ordered it in August 1930). Only the radio station remained in full operation. Cigarettes replaced cigars and a disease threatened the local sponge activity. On July 1, 1934 Key West officially declared insolvency and threw itself into the hands of the state. The 1935 state census showed the population of Key West as 13,118 and the remainder of the Keys as 865. In 1945 the population was 19,755.

The state was no better off than Key West and neither was the country. So it was up to President Franklin Roosevelt and his New Deal programs with acronyms such as the CWA, WPA, PWA, CCC, and FERA. Julius Stone headed the Florida division of the Federal Emergency Relief Administration (FERA) in Jacksonville, but he found special favor in Key West. It appears that he spent more time in Key West than the rest of Florida and Key West realized the benefits. Many programs were started and continued through the Works Progress Administration (WPA) period. One project was the Key West Aquarium besides Mallory Dock which was started in 1933.

As if things were not bad enough, the Hurricane of 1935 cut Key West off from the mainland. Forty miles of railroad were destroyed in the Upper Keys and Key West was back to depending on maritime transportation. Some degree of help was provided by the new industry of air transportation. Temporary vehicle ferry landings were provided and two Mississippi River stern-wheelers were converted to link Key West to the mainland. Fortunately, Key West possessed a great harbor and was accustomed to living by the sea. For the more fortunate, Pan American Airways had just established regular service between Miami and Key West. On a smaller scale, in November 1935 the Thompson Fish Company purchased the

Overseas Transportation Company as a freight service since the railroad was destroyed.

The damaged railroad right-of-way and bridges were converted to what I call the second Overseas Highway. The narrow railroad bridges were widened to 20-foot two-lane vehicle bridges. It was completed in 1938 and one could for the first time drive all the way to and from Key West without the use of car ferries. A gala highway celebration took place of the weekend of July 2-4 and Bernice Brantlt, Miss Key West, served as the queen, Visitors, delivery trucks and buses frequented all the principal Keys.

The new highway opening Key West to and from the nation was brought to national attention when on February 18, 1939, President Franklin Roosevelt passed through the Upper Keys in route to Key West to board the cruiser *Houston* to observe war games in the Caribbean. Poor Ole Craig waved to the entourage when in passed through Craig Key in an open convertible at about 2 p.m. Key West mayor, Willard

Albury, met the president at the west end of the Bahia Honda bridge on West Summerland Key. From there, Mayor Albury accompanied the president to tour much of the then inactive naval facilities. Former Florida F.E.R.A./W.P.A. director Julius Stone's 1934 exhortation to Key West of its tourist potential was now a reality. The Gibraltar of the South had a usable vehicle artery to and from the mainland

World War II

In early 1941 Paramount Studios had photographers in Key West filming scenes for the future movie "Reap the Wild Wind." As with most of the nation, WW-II lifted Key West out of its sagging economy. President Roosevelt had driven the converted Overseas Highway and visited Key West in 1939. On October 14, 1939, Navy Headquarters announced the closed Navy Station would reopen November 1. The same year the Navy signed a contract for Trumbo Point for use as a Naval Air Station. The first spade full of dirt was turned on

March 12, 1940. The base served as an training and operating base for the U.S. Navy's fleet aircraft squadrons. The Navy was back in Key West and no one knew what would happen a little more than a year later.

One such valuable military resources at Key West was the Fleet Sonar School at the naval station in 1940. The school was invaluable for training sonar operators for the country's struggle against German U-boats a few years later. Pearl Harbor occurred almost two years later. The country was at war again. The sonar school closed in the early 1970s. The Key West economy was damaged when a mysterious blight attacked the sponges. The sponges disintegrated when touched by the retrieving hook.

In summary, once again Key West was on a military economy. Without all the details, World War II expanded the naval operations from around 50 acres to over 3,000 acres, including Boca Chica. It took over the old F.E.C. Trumbo Point railroad yard and improved

Sigsbee Park. In March 1945 one naval operational entity was established - U.S. Naval Air Station, Key West. The Fleet Sonar School was in full operation. About 15,000 military personnel supported these operations. After WW-II the navy retained its training facilities.

The needs of the Navy in Key West helped all the Keys. To support its wartime mission the Navy needed fresh water, so it paid for an 18-inch pipeline the length of the Keys. Equipment was larger and heavier so an improved highway was made. A total of 17 miles was cutoff by eliminating the out-of-the-way route via Pirates Cove and up to present day Ocean Reef. Since federal funds were used, Highway US-1 was born. Its route is the one we drive today. (Public water and electricity are on separate web pages.)

After WW-II, the whole country increased in mobility. New churches and schools sprang into life. Things were not all peaches and ice cream as in the summer of 1946 Key West suffered it worst polio epidemic ever.

Twenty cases were reported with two deaths. Restrictions barred children under 16 from public places. Mosquito control was put into effect as a county agency in 1951. At first it was spraying with trucks but by 1960 the Beech type 18 aircraft were used. All the elements for growth were present. But the economy of Key West was once again on the wane. The free-spirited sailors that were on liberty went back to their homes to regain their lost time. The US Navy was again down sizing. 1951 was not a dull year for Key West as as the 1000-unit Navy housing project on former Dredger's Island was renamed Sigsbee Park. Navy Captain Sigsbee was the captain of the USS Maine sank in the harbor of of Havana in 1898. The old Army barracks on Palm Avenue was named Peary Court after the discoverer of the North Pole. Incidentally, at this time tourism was ranked fourth.

Here is something for some one to check out for a "first." In January 1953 the Key West Citizen reported that Edmond Albury acquired a building permit to construct on Eaton Street a CBS house - just wondering? Another marker of growth in March of 1953 the 6,000th telephone was installed on the switchboard to the home of Lt. F. E. Mitschke. The same year the county's population was reported as 29,975. I do not have the exact numbers, but Key West would have been about 26,500. Both Key West and the remainder of the county was growing fast. A strange weather event occurred on October 12 when the Key West Weather Bureau reported a record low of 64 degrees.

However, in September of 1955 the lack of summer tourists prompted a "motel price war" and eight motels offered free rooms to tourists. In November of 1955 the U.S. Navy presented a breakdown of its Key West population: 936 officers, 9,000 enlisted personnel, 6,661 dependents and 1,725 civil service for a total of 18,322. The civilian population was 26,433. Things were not that bad as Stock Island had it first stock car race. There 17 local and 19 Miami car drivers.

Pink Gold

The economy of Key West was saved again when 'pink gold' was found in the Marquesas and Tortugas areas in 1949. This was a new commercial variety of shrimp considered delicious, large and pink with fine flavoring. As with once popular Key West cigars, now there were the 'Key West Pinks.' Shrimp boats numbered around 500 in the winters which was the best season for shrimp. In 1953 the tradition of today's Mallory Square was innocently started when the Key West Motor Court Association petitioned the city for use as a public fishing pier. The 1960 census showed Key West's population at 33,956, more that two time the remainder of the county at 13,965 - a total of 47,921.

The Key West NAS responded to the 1962 Cuban Missile Crisis when on October 22, 1962 reconnaissance flight began to support the Cuban blockade. After the short burst of activity caused by the Cuban Missile Crisis, the military in Key West continued to down size. Destroyer Squadron 12 and

Submarine Squadron 12 were decommissioned at a joint ceremony on June 29, 1973 signaling the beginning of the end. On March 29, 1974, Admiral John Maurer ordered his flag lowered terminating 151 years of naval operations at the Key West Naval Station. Navy Lt. Mathew Perry had raised the American flag on March 24, 1822. Naval air operations continued however, and U. S. Coast Guard operations were expanding.

When the military down sizes there is a related loss of civilian jobs. To some, the 1970s correlated with the rum running days of the 1920s and 30s. Even though rum running and drug running are similar in actions, the reaction were quite different. Key West had to look back to Julius Stone who in 1934 told them that they were missing a gold mine as the the "Gibraltar of the US." A century earlier Commodore Porter compared Key West to Gibraltar. The city fathers and businessmen made historic Key West into a thriving tourist center to their credit without destroying their tangible legacy. Not to be forgotten is that the county seat's local government's economy provides some stability to Key West's economy.

Tourism is fickle as in May 1880 the Chamber of Commerce asked the governor to declare the city an economic disaster because of the adverse impact of the Cuban boat lift mainly from bad media coverage. Intelligence reported up to 100,000 Muriel refugees awaiting to come to Florida. The U.S. Coast Guard began its largest peacetime operation by ordering additional cutters for the area. To add to the problem a 73 mph squall line passed through the straits killing an estimated 12 refugees. The same year Governor Bob Graham concluded that hurricane sheltering in the Keys was "clearly insufficient" and residents should be evacuated in case of hurricanes. Tourism was now firmly entrenched. Even the old small "southernmost sign" (often stolen by collectors) was replaced with a new and larger concrete marker in 1983.

The U.S. Border Patrol established a road block near Florida City to check the citizenship of everyone leaving the Keys on April 18, 1982. Traffic was being backed for 15 miles or more and legitimate visitors were reluctant to come. On April 22, 1982 Key West took the lead by forming the Conch Republic and symbolically seceding from the Union. Symbolic border passes and visas were issued. Wooden Conch currency was sold, the pelican was declared the Republic's bird and then hibiscus the flower. The Conch Republic went as far as applying for foreign aid.

The Conclusion

Like a military economy, a tourist economy is unpredictable, something that Florida well knows, but of which it often looses sight. Almost weekly the city debates the dichotomy of huge cruise ships docked near groups of homeless sleeping in the neighborhoods. A knee-jerk in the world economy can be a blow to the head for tourism, but fortunately these blips are usually short lived. An example was the

1974 gasoline shortage. A political knee-jerk can likewise bring prosperity. Key West, as well as the other Keys, have survived about every kind of calamity except earthquakes and avalanches. They will survive others in the future, that is unless global warming becomes a reality with rising sea levels.

Key West City, Florida USA

Key West Travel and Tourism
Quick Guide

Climate

Key West claims to be the only city in the lower 48 states never to have had a frost. Because of the proximity of the Gulf Stream in the Straits of Florida, about 12 miles (19 km) south and southeast, and the tempering effects of the Gulf of Mexico to the west and north, Key West has a notably mild, semi-tropical climate, though, due to the islands being slightly above the Tropic of Cancer, it is not truly tropical. in the wintertime, cold snaps, occasionally, bring temperatures in the 40's to the islands .

Precipitation is characterized by dry and wet seasons. The period of November through April receives abundant sunshine and slightly less than 25 percent of the annual rainfall. This rainfall usually occurs in advance of cold fronts in a few heavy or light showers. May through October is normally the wet season, receiving approximately 53 percent of the yearly total in numerous showers and thunderstorms. Rain falls on most days of the wet season. Early morning is the favored time for these showers, which is different from mainland Florida, where showers and thunderstorms usually occur in the afternoon. Easterly (tropical) waves during this season occasionally bring excessive rainfall, while infrequent hurricanes may be accompanied by unusually heavy amounts. At any rate, Key West is the driest city in Florida.

Getting in
By plane

Key West International Airport (IATA: EYW) (ICAO: KEYW), 3491 South Roosevelt Blvd., (305) 296-7223, Served by several airlines, though a short runway prevents big jets from landing. Direct flights are available from Atlanta, Charlotte, most major cities in Florida, and also some flights to the Bahamas. Fares tend to be quite high. A popular route to fly in is via Miami International Airport or Fort Lauderdale International Airport.

If you plan to rent a car, be aware that both Enterprise and Alamo desks are not located at the airport. You have to call the shuttle bus and wait for 12 min to catch a ride to the Truman Av. location.

By bus

Traveling from Miami Beach to Key West is now possible every day. Tours depart from Miami Beach every day at 6:30AM. Travel in comfort across the Overseas Highway and 7-Mile Bridge. On this tour, you'll get to do some sightseeing in Key West and spend approximately 6 hours in Key West. You will be able to explore the island on your own pace.

Key West Full Day Tour, 305-894-6409, Take a day tour from Miami Beach to Key West and travel across 43 bridges and 31 islands down the Florida Keys to Key West. Once in Key West, experience a tropical atmosphere complete with street artists, outdoor cafes and shops. "From.

Xcursions USA, 786-299-9261 (toll free: 1 888 884-6934), a Miami based provider of Luxury motorcoach tour and sightseeing services that provides daily ground transportation Miami - Key West - Miami.

Greyhound, 3535 S Roosevelt, Suite #104 (*Key West Airport*), 305-296-9072 (toll free: 1-800-231-2222), Travels primarily on US-1 between Miami (3 stops) & Key West via Key Largo, Islamorada, Marathon Key and Big Pine Key. Passengers transfer to other buses in Miami and Orlando to get to other cities. Transfer to the 'Blue' or 'Green' Line bus from the airport/greyhound terminal into town.

Keys Shuttle, 305 289-9997 (toll free: 1 888 765-9997). The company provides door-to-door service between the Keys and the Miami and Ft. Lauderdale-Hollywood International Airports.

MiamiToKeyWestBus.com, Mel Fisher Museum @ 200 Greene St (*Wi-Fi and Restroom on Board*), 305-423-9045, Direct motorcoach transportation services to Key West from Miami. Attractions in Key West. From $29.

Series of Public Buses, The Lower Keys Shuttle operated by Key West Transit provides nine trips per day between MM 0 in Key West and MM 52.5 in Marathon Key . The fare is $4 for the Lower Keys Shuttle. At Marathon,MM50, transfer to the Miami-Dade bus route 301 , Dade/Monroe Express that offers 6 trips daily between approx. 8AM and 11PM to the Florida City Wal-Mart. From the Florida city Wal-Mart, take the #38 bus (Busway Max) to the Dadeland South

(Metro Rail) Station to catch the train into Miami. The Dade/Monroe express costs $2.35 each way.

FREE Duval Loop Bus provides service every 15 minutes until midnight, 7 days per week in the immediate downtown Key West area.

By train
Amtrak takes you as far south as the Miami Airport Station. From there transfer to the Keys Shuttle onwards. See above. Amtrak: 1-800-USARAIL. There are NO trains to or in Key West.

By sea
Key West Express This company operates daily high-speed passenger ferries from Ft. Myers Beach and Marco Island. The ferries dock at the Key West Bight Ferry Terminal in the heart of the Historic Seaport District with its many fine restaurants, bars and shops. Passengers can walk to Duval Street, the heart of old town Key West, in about 15 minutes. The ferry ride takes approximately 3.5 hours and the Ft. Myers Beach vessels has a capacity exceeding 450 passengers and

amenities aboard include; out-door sundecks, flat-screen TV's, galley service and a full bar. Additionally, the Marco Island vessel features the same amenities along with a capacity of over 250 passengers.

<u>Private Boaters</u> Experienced boaters can navigate to Key West along the Atlantic side of the Keys or by traveling on the Gulf of Mexico side. The first part of the trip takes you through the specially-marked Intracoastal Waterway. After Long Key, however, international markers apply. Consult the appropriate Coast Pilot and Light List manuals. Numerous marinas are waiting to entertain you, but you should make reservations ahead.

<u>Cruise Ships</u> In 1969 the Port of Key West received its first regularly scheduled cruise ship. The three docking facilities -- Mallory Square Dock, Pier B (privately owned by Westin), and the Navy Mole (aka Outer Mole) -- service over half a million passengers a year. Mallory Square Dock and Pier B are right in the heart of town; Navy Mole is on military property however your

ship should provide chartered trolleys to take you to Mallory Square. A schedule indicating when a particular cruise ship will be calling on Key West is available at the Port Office and online.

Currently, there are NO international ferries to the Caribbean or the Yucatan Peninsula in Mexico. Closest thing would be the cruise ship excursions to the foreign port of cal and back. See above or contact the cruise ship company.

By car
The Overseas Highway terminates in Key West, and links all the towns in the Keys with mainland Florida, which provides links into the US Interstate network, so driving to Key West is straightforward (3 1/2 hours or 170mi/272km from Miami along US-1), though driving around town can be difficult and long-term parking may be expensive.

From Miami International Airport: Take LeJeune Road south to 836 West. Follow the Florida Turnpike south toward Key West. The Turnpike ends at US 1 in Florida

City. Follow U.S. 1 south as far as it goes and you will be in Key West.

From Ft. Lauderdale-Hollywood International Airport: Exit the airport and follow the signs for 595 West. Take 595 to the Florida Turnpike and follow the signs for the Florida Keys and Key WEST.

From the north: take the Florida Turnpike south and follow the signs for Homestead and Key West. The Florida Turnpike ends at US 1 in Florida City.Follow U.S. 1 south into the Florida Keys.

From Florida's West Coast: take I-75 Alligator Alley east to the Miami exit, and south to the Turnpike Extension.

By boat
The Key West Express leaves several time a week from Fort Myers Beach. It departs year round on all days except those indicated on calendar on the site . Trips from Marco Island departs seasonally December through April.

Getting around

Driving around Key West is difficult and parking is expensive. (Although there is free parking in front of the USS *Mohawk* Museum, at the intersection of Southard St and Fort St.) Really, you don't actually need a car to get around Key West if you plan to stick to the island. Many visitors choose to rent motor scooters, bicycles, golf carts or explore on foot. When renting a golf cart keep in mind that you have to find parking for this vehicle as well. Scooters and bikes can normally be parked on the sidewalk right outside your destination. However, really consider insuring anything you rent. Driving is recommended and necessary if planning to stop or stay anywhere along the Keys from Sugarloaf Key to Florida City.

The main street in Key West is Duval street.

Key West has a tram system that gives tours of most areas of the island. And Key West has the most bicycle friendly weather/climate in the world. Just remember;

drink plenty of fluids, wear light weight, light colored clothing, and don't forget the sunscreen either.

There is a fairly comprehensive bus system with color-coded lines . Unlimited travel tickets are available for periods between 7 days and a month and are good value.

Fares: (Discounts are available for senior citizens, students etc.)
Single Trip: $2
7-Day $8/Unlimited Use
31-Day $25

If you plan to rent a car be aware that both Enterprise and Alamo desks are not located at the airport. You have to call the shuttle bus and wait for 12 minutes to catch a ride to the Truman Ave location. Budget is the only car rental agency in Key West that does not charge additional fees (usually $10/day from anyone else) for a second driver -- so if you are traveling with a partner who drives, be advised.

One Key West Taxi Service is reached at 1-305-295-5555. Uber and Lyft ride-sharing services became available in Key West last year.

Seeing

Southernmost point in continental United States

<u>Key West AIDS Memorial</u>, White Street and Atlantic Boulevard *on the beach*. The City of Key West has lost more than a thousand of its citizens to the AIDS epidemic. Some of their names are inscribed on a memorial near the White Street Pier. The memorial is embedded in the sidewalk near the ocean, and made of flat smooth granite. The memorial was dedicated on World AIDS Day in 1997, and funded entirely through private sources. At the time of dedication, there were 730 names engraved on the memorial. There are spaces for 1,500 names, and each year more are added and dedicated in a ceremony, also on World AIDS Day in December. A group called Friends of the Key West AIDS Memorial takes care of the memorial.

Key West City, Florida USA

<u>Key West City Cemetery</u> In Key West, burial customs reflect combinations of African, Hispanic, Anglo and other mixed heritages. Due to the water table of the Keys, most burials are in above ground tombs. Grave markers with unusual inscriptions such as *I told you I was sick*, *Devoted* Fan *of Julio Iglesias* and *At Least I know where he's sleeping tonight* are not unusual. Cemetery maps are available at the front gate.

<u>Wildlife Rescue of the Florida Keys</u>, Atlantic Boulevard and White Streets.

<u>McCoy Indigenous Park</u> is the setting for this rescue operation in Key West that has released more than 2,000 healed animals into the wild since 1993. They take care of any animal that needs attention, from sea birds to raccoons, and at any given time you might see up to 100 creatures healing at the center. They come from all over, from the Seven Mile bridge to the Dry Tortugas. You can visit the patients any day from 9AM to 5PM, and the park is open sunup to sundown. It's free, but they like donations and volunteers.

Southernmost Point, Corner of Whitehead and South Streets. The southernmost point in the continental USA.

Shipwreck Museum, 1 Whitehead St., (305) 292-8990 (Fax: (305) 292-1617), Offers a panoramic view of the island from its observation tower.

Key West Lighthouse, 938 Whitehead Street, Open daily from 9:30AM-4:30PM. With a panoramic view of the island. Adults $10, Students/Seniors $9, Children $5, under 6 free.

Key West Maps (*Key West Maps*), Although the island of Key West is only 2 x 4 Miles, it is quite possible to get lost. You can find printed maps of the island and its attractions at most gas stations. If you have a smartphone try using these interactive maps of Key West. They provide the locations of just about everything on the island including various restaurants and attractions you may be looking for.

Doing

Key West is a great place for the family. There is plenty to do during the day...for those that are awake. Enjoy an early night and prepare for the next day's adventure. However, if you are traveling with young ones, stay in a hotel off the main streets. For those who stay out all night you may not get to do these things but you should try. Be aware that the beaches in Key West are average at best. Many of the beaches are very small, made up of hard, dredged sand, and are not natural. They are not bad, per se, but if you are expecting Miami Beach caliber, you will be sorely disappointed.

<u>Sunset Watersports</u>, phone="855-378-6386" url="http://sunsetwatersportskeywest.com/" Sunset Watersports is Key West Florida's premier water sports company. Offering: Parasailing, Snorkeling Trips, All Day Watersports Adventures, Jet Ski Tours, Boat Rentals, Sunset Cruise and Sunset Sail, Dolphin Trips, Safari Speed Boat Trips, Dinner Cruises, Key West

Smathers Beach Passes. Sunset Watersports offers a "Do It All" option, 12 watersport activities for 6 hours of fun. As Key West Florida's Oldest water sports company we can offer you the best experience on the water.

<u>Key West Nature Preserve</u> Two entrances on Atlantic Blvd., Ocean front property that has been turned into an accessible natural area. Enjoy seeing local Key West wildlife such as lizard butterflies and maybe even a snake.

<u>Astro City</u> Atlantic Blvd. A popular stop for families on their way to and from the beach. Located directly across the street from Higgs beach.

<u>Florida Keys Eco-Discovery Center</u>, Truman Annex Waterfront. With its touch screens, stunning photos, and roomy theater showing a short high-definition film about the Keys ecosystems, this educational center has become a hit with families. It's a fun way to learn about reef and mangrove habitats before or after an

excursion. The newest addition is the Living Reef exhibit, which features a 2,500-gallon reef aquarium. Free admission and parking on-site.

Ghosts and Legends of Key West, 90 minute walking tour of Old Key West. "Old Town Key West" Area. The most informative and historically correct versions of Key West ghost lore.

Sebago Watersports, Waterfront Area, Reef snorkeling, sunset sails and much more. All things water. Sebago trips are always full of fun and a wonderful crew that will take good care of you. Sunset sails, para-sailing, all day adventures from the tame *Island Ting* to the active *Power Adventure*. The para-sailing tends to be a bit brief (13 minutes), but the crew is friendly.

Dry Tortugas National Park, Details daily trips to Fort Jefferson. By ferry with Yankee Freedom II

Swim With Dolphins, for ages 5 and older. Key Largo / Key West Area.

Conch Tour Train, 201 Front Street, 305-294-5161, The World Famous Conch Train sightseeing tour of Key West focuses on the historic Old Town area of the island. Highlights include the Hemingway House, Mallory Square, Duval Street and the Historic Seaport. Stops in Mallory Square and the Historic Seaport.

Glass Bottom Boat, Snorkel, and Dolphin watch, For ages 5 and older. Key West/ Key West Area.

Diving in Key West, Offering Daily Dive trips to the reefs near Key West.

Sunset Watercraft, Key West offers a host of sightseeing opportunities, including romantic sunset cruises. At Cow Key Marina on Stock Island. Reasonable prices for the 28 mile round-the-island jet ski run (1.5 hours). The jet skis themselves are a bit beat up, but the motors hum right along at high speed. Guides are safe and knowledgeable, but give the renter plenty of rope to enjoy.

Key West Fishing, Offers charters, guides, and fishing information for Key West. Includes private and group fishing charters.

Sunset Celebration, at Mallory Square in Key West (where Duval Street meets the Gulf of Mexico). This event begins every evening a few hours before sunset and is much like a street carnival, with vendors, performers, food, and fun. Also a great photo op for some of the most beautiful sunsets.

Trails of Margaritaville Tour, Jimmy Buffett spent his "formative" years in Key West, and this tour will regale you with tales of those days. I suspect you'll hear some Semi-True Stories (believe it or not), but it's a good time for Parrotheads and non-Buffett fans alike.

The Southernmost Scavenger Hunt Phone (305)292-9994 Since winning the prestigious "Venture Award" from the Key West Chamber of Commerce, The Southernmost Scavenger Hunt has expanded to offer a wider variety of custom designed features to their ever-popular scavenger hunts. Participants are able to enjoy all the sights and sounds that make the "Southernmost City" such an unforgettable destination.

Fury Water Adventures, Fury Water Adventures is a water sports company that has been in Key West for almost the past three decades. It offers snorkeling, para-sailing, jet skiing, kayaking, rock climbing, water trampoline, sunset sails and cruises, reef eco tours, and glass bottom boat tours. Fury also offers combo packages such as the Ultimate Adventure, the Rum & Reggae, and the Commotion on the Ocean.

Ernest Hemingway House, 907 Whitehead Street, 9AM-5PM daily. Hemingway lived and wrote here for a decade. He also raised cats, the descendants of which still roam the grounds and have extra toes. $12.

Restless Native Charters, (*Key West bight marina at historic waterfront seaport*), 305-394-0600, Luxury sailing catamaran for sail/dive, sunset sails, private partys, weddings/proposals. Upscale food and drink and a great adventure on the water.

Dolphin Tours (*Wild About Dolphins*), 6000 Peninsular Ave, Stock Island FL (*Key West Harbour Yacht Club*), 305-294-5026, An absolutely wonderful private boat tour to snorkel and dolphins sightings. Capt. Sherry is the best!

Harry S. Truman Little White House, 111 Front St., A historic retreat used by President Harry S. Truman. Guided tours are available, as well as a gift shop. It's still used as a retreat and place of business by US government officials today.

Honest Works Island Pottery co, 929 Truman Ave (*mile marker 1*), 4193089221, 9 - 6. Honest Works Island Pottery Co. is a vibrant art gallery and active studio space in Old town Key West. Stop on by and watch the pottery in the making or make it yourself. Honest Works offers pottery classes, as well as, paint your own pottery for locals and tourist alike. In this dynamic studio space artists, Adam Russell and Kelly Lever, create and display their own colorful island pottery. Come on in and fell the artist energy flowing!

<u>Fort Zachary Taylor</u>, 601 Howard England Way (*end of Southard Street on Truman Annex*), 3052920037, 8AM - sundown. The perfect romantic place to cuddle up with someone special, unwind, and watch the sun set as sailboats glide by...all without the crazy circus of Mallory Square. It doesn't get any more romantic in this crowded city. Nature trails, 1866 fort with a real moat, beaches, snack stand. $6-8.

<u>Key West Pub Crawl</u> (*Duval Crawl*), 218 Whitehead Street #2 (*Corner of Whitehead & Greene*), 305-294-7170, 8pm. Key West is famous for its bars- day or night the pubs are always rocking. Are you looking for the ultimate Key West tradition? Come along and do the "Duval Crawl," a 2.5 hour guided tour offered Tuesday and Friday nights at 8PM. 5 cocktails and a souvenir t-shirt are included. price listed is for those

who book online. regular price is $35.00 a person. $29.95.

Southernmost Bike Tour, 218 Whitehead Street, 305-849-2706, 8am - 8pm. Join your knowledgeable local guide for a leisurely ride through Historic Key West. Your two hour adventure includes the use of a comfortable beach cruiser bicycle, safety helmet and a complimentary bottle of water. On the tour you will visit numerous points of interest such as Truman Annex, the Southernmost Point, White Street Pier and the Key West Cemetery. Your route will take you down picturesque Old Town streets lined with tropical foliage, past famous homes and stunning gardens. Don't forget your camera, sunglasses and comfortable shoes! $34.95.

Ocean Vue Adventure (*Key West Snorkel, Glassbottom Boat and Dolphin Encounter*), 201 William St., (305) 851-5788, 9 - 5. Ocean Vue Adventures is the local 3-in-1 tour, where guests can enjoy a glassbottom boat ride and see all the sea creatures on the way out to the coral reef for a great snorkel, then venture out to see the dolphins play in their natural habitat.

Improomptu Classical Concerts, St. Paul's Espiscopal Church (*Eaton and Duval Sts. Key West*), Six classical "chamber" concerts on Sunday afternoons at 4pm during January, February and March.

Festivals

- ✓ Fantasy Fest, Annual event. Will next be held October 23 - November 1, 2015.
- ✓ Gay Spring Break. Annual event held in February, March, and April targeting college-age LGBT students.
- ✓ Womenfest, Annual event Will next be held September 4 - 9, 2012. One of the largest lesbian-oriented parties on earth!
- ✓ Tropical Heat, Adult-themed event for gay men held every year. Will next be held August 16 - 19, 2012.

- ✓ Lobsterfest Held every year around the first week in August. This year: August 10 - 12, 2012.

Buying

Key West is not like Miami. There are very few high end shops or big name brands. While there are a few, Key West is not the place for this type of shopping. Fly into or out of the Miami airport and spend a day in South Beach if this is what you are looking for. There are a lot of shops in Key West, especially along Duval Street. You can find something to wear at night which in Key West isn't much (price or material). Lose your sunglasses...they have them. Need suntan lotion..check. Want a tattoo? You could get probably get 20 or so if you went to every tattoo place in Key West. This is not a good idea if you have been drinking. You may regret it the next sober morning when you realize you have one or more.

Blue, 718 Caroline St, A boutique specializing in women's clothing. Everything from fun tees, to comfy linen pants they have everything for a casual day of drinking.

Fairvilla Megastore, 520 Front Street, *across from the Pier House*, Phone: *+1 305* 292-0448, Intimate apparel, exotic fashions, sensual accessories, romantic gifts, playful novelties, passionate books and tantalizing movies! M-Sa 9AM-2AM, Su 10AM-2AM.

Key Lime-N-More, 424 Greene Street, *Next door to* Captain *Tony's Saloon*, Phone: *+1 305* 296-9515, All things Key Lime. The only home made Key Lime pie on the island. Friendly shopkeepers that treat you as more than just another tourist. Hours vary.

Conch Republic Gifts A gift store offering Conch Republic-related items including flags, shirts, magnets and more.

Paradise Tattoo, 627 Duval St., 305-292-9110, 10AM-10PM, 7 Days. What better way to remember your trip to Key West than with a permanent souvenir? Paradise

Tattoo is Key West's Largest, Cleanest & Oldest Studio. So come on get stuck in Paradise.

Bare Bones Beach Shop, inc., 2770 N. Roosevelt Blvd. (*Overseas Market next to Winn-Dixie*), 305-296-5970, 9am-6pm Mon-Sat. Bare Bones Beach Shop has swimwear and beach products for men, women and children, in addition to stylish dog clothing and accessories. mid.

7 Artists & Friends (*nearly 100% Local Art*), 122 Duval Street (*Just 2 blocks from cruise ship dock*), 305.294.8444, 10am-10pm. 7 Artists & Friends represents many of Key West's favorite artists. Come in and check out the fresh caught local art. Photo realism, sculpture, jewelry, abstract, watercolor, photography, whimsy and glass; this gallery has it all.

Eating

Yellofin Bar & Grill, 5950 Peninsular Avenue, Key West FL 33040, 305-809-8204, Dine on Florida's legendary seafood and Caribbean-influenced cuisine at Yellowfin

Bar & Grill, featuring handcrafted furniture, industrial flair and laid-back atmosphere combine with the waterfront views and al fresco dining in Key West.

Budget

Conch Republic, 631 Greene Street. Enjoy their spacious waterfront setting where the atmosphere is like a trip back in time to the way Key West used to be. Enjoy fresh fish and a raw bar. Feel like you are dining outside with the large windows that remain open during the day. A great place for a drink & some snacks specially during football season.

El Siboney, 900 Catherine Street, *+1 305* 296 4184. This Cuban restaurant, tucked into a quiet residential intersection, flies well below the tourist radar. Delicious food at very reasonable prices. To sum it up, this is where the locals go for Cuban.

Jimmy Buffett's Margaritaville, 500 Duval Street, *+1 305* 292-1435. Key West is pretty close to paradise, so you might as well have a cheeseburger while you're there. Prices are not overly high. Less than 4 bucks for a Cheeseburger in Paradise.

<u>Schooner Wharf</u>, Caroline Street, a surprising choice for breakfast, this rough and ready landmark has a three-egg seafood omelette that, coupled with a Bloody Mary or two, will shock you back to life from a throw down night on Duval.

<u>Mam's Best Food</u>, 405 Petronia Street (between Duval and Whitehead), (305) 896-0923. Key West's only Glatt Kosher eatery (closed Friday afternoon and all day Saturday). Authentic home-cooked Israeli food. Hebrew spoken. The falafel and mezze are popular with local "Goyim" as well as visiting Jews.

<u>BO's Fish Wagon</u>, 801 Caroline St Key West, FL 33040, (305) 294-9272. This is an open air shack that sells food, beer/wine, and has music on Friday nights. Check it out when you are headed towards Turtle Krawls from Duval Street. As seen via Bobby Flay on The Food

Network. You will see license plates from previous customers adorning the spaces.

Mid-range

A & B Lobster House 700 Front St, The main dishes are mid-range in price paired with great tasting and priced appetizers and salads it will be hard to forget your meal here. While Key West is warm and the porch may seem like a good idea make sure the ladies have jackets. It is right on the water and with the fans on high blast it can get a little chilly.

Mangia-Mangia Pasta, 900 Southard St, *+1* 305 294-2469, Every day 5:30PM-10PM.

El Meson de Pepe, 410 Wallstreet, Mallory Square, *+1 305* 295-2620, If you want authentic, delicious Cuban food look nor further. I have been visiting this place for about the last 5 years when I drive down to Key West. Be ready for a special treat on the days that Pepe himself takes over the kitchen and creates his delectable masterpieces. The prices are very reasonable and their Mojitos have a kick. Every night at Sunset, they have a band playing and enough space for dancing and having a couple of drinks at the bar.

<u>Roof Top Cafe</u> Exactly what the names suggest, this is a restaurant situated on the roof top of a building. Overlooking Mallory square this place is perfect for dining during sunset or under the stars. As well as dinner they also serve Breakfast and lunch. Nothing is too expensive and the food is of good quality.

<u>The Half Shell Raw Bar</u> Phone: (305)294-7496 231 Margaret St. A Taste of Old Key West! Traditional Key West Raw Bar & great Key West seafood restaurant! Oysters, clams, shrimp, more! A low key restaurant for casual lunch or dinner. Settle down to an informal atmosphere, local characters, great bar and waterfront dining. It's a little piece of Old Key West on the historic Key West Bight. Drop in! Enjoy a frosty drink and the freshest seafood this side of the reef!

Splurge

<u>Nine One Five</u>, 915 Duval Street. Dinner served from 6PM-11PM. With weather so nice you want to spend as much time outside as possible. So why not take your dining outside...or as close as possible? Join others on the porch of this dignified Victorian home. Similar to tapas dining, everything is intended to be shared and mixed and matched.

<u>Seven Fish</u>, 632 Olivia St., *+1 305* 296-2777, This very small restaurant tucked away on Olivia St, is a true delight. The staff is intelligent and polite, the fish dishes are always fresh and innovative. Reservations a must.

<u>Square One</u>, 1075 Duval St # C12, *+1 305* 296-4300, They serve breakfast lunch dinner and even Sunday brunch. The menu is very similar to many other restaurants. A lot of fish and seafood. A lot of "tropical' flavors and many fruits are included in the ingredients of their dishes.

Louie's Backyard, 700 Waddell Avenue. One of Key West's finest restaurants with gourmet preparations, including their signature dish of shrimp and grits. Large oceanfront deck is popular with locals and visitors during sunset.

Drink

There are a large number of drinking establishments of various types. The main tourist strip on Duval Street has numerous watering holes.

Bourbon Street Pub, 724 Duval St, *+1 305*294-9354, Part of the gay-oriented Bourbon St. Complex on the 700 block of Duval.

Captain Tony's Saloon, 428 Greene Street, Ernest Hemingway's old stomping grounds. Pirate's Punch in a 22 oz cup.

Fat Tuesdays, 305 Duval St., *+1 305*296-9373, So you're not in New Orleans...who says that means you can't have Mardi Gras! Featured on MTV's Real World Key West here it is Mardi Gras everyday. Fat Tuesdays is a frozen drink bar most known for their mixed daiquiri's. The bar features a range of drinks from classics like margaritas to twisted combinations that mix the flavors of several frozen drink recipes. They also offer a special that includes discounted refills when you purchase their Fat Tuesdays souviner bottles.

<u>Hog's Breath Saloon</u>, 400 Front Street, *+1 305*292-2032 (email:), Take a peek at the "hog cam" on their site.

<u>Irish Kevin's Pub</u>, 211-C Duval Street, *+1 305*292-1262, Webcams here, too. Can be a lively place at times. They often offer live music and even sell Irish Kevin's merchandise which can be a great souviner if you visit around St. Patricks day!

<u>The Lazy Gecko Bar</u> 203 Duval St, Next door to Sloppy Joe's bar. This place offers air conditioning if you can't take the heat. Also cool off with one of their 12 daiquiris. Hungry? Grab a slice of pizza or a fresh sandwich. Starting early...join The Lazy gecko for happy

hour from 5-8. Like your friends a lot? Rent the whole place!

Rick's/Durty Harry's Entertainment, 202 Duval St., Complex offers it all! Key West's #1 Club w/ 6 different venues & 10 bars. Best live entertainment, VIP bar overlooking the action, famous juice & premium spirits bar, hottest dance club, premier adult entertainment, & best live Rock & Roll! They also offer many drink specials most popular is the 3 hour unlimited drinks from 8-11pm for just $10.

Sloppy Joe's Bar, 201 Duval St, *+1* 305 294-8759, Ernest Hemingway's "new" stomping grounds. Sloppy Joe's used to sit at the current location of Captain Tony's, but the landlord raised the rent on the owner back in 1937. Legend has it that upon hearing the news, the bar owner and his customers (including Hemingway) moved the bar, barstools, alcohol, etc. across Duval Street to a former restaurant - its current location.

There are also plenty of places to wet your whistle that aren't necessarily right on Duval Street.

Green Parrot Bar, 601 Whitehead St, *+1 305* 294-6133, The last (or first, depending on your direction of travel) bar on US 1. Not your typical trop-rock bar, the Green Parrot leans more toward blues. Great bands, and an unbelievable selection of blues on the jukebox. Just remember, no snivelers.

Rum Barrel Tavern, 528 Front St, *+1 305* 292-7862, Pat Croce's place features the largest selection of rums in the world. Not a rum drinker? Plenty of other libations to be had. Several big-screen TVs (you'll never miss an event involving a Philadelphia team) and a deck overlooking Old Town.

Schooner Wharf Bar, 202 William St, *+1 305* 294-3302, A last little piece of Old Key West, Schooner Wharf is an open air bar that sits on the Key West Bight. Grab a brew and watch the yachts.

Finnegans Wake 320 Grinnell St Celebrate life in true Irish Style.

Bogarts Irish Pub, 900 - 904 Duval Street, Key West, 305-296-0815, An Irish pub and restaurant attached to a bed and breakfast located right on Duval Street. Daily happy hour specials offered as well as great Irish food. Come in and say hi and enjoy a nice cold pint.

Kokomo Joe's Off Duval Bar Crawl, 422 Fleming St (*crawl starts at Agave 308 on Front St*), (305)731-9630 tix 800 979-3370, 3. Pub Crawl off the beaten tourist path. "Zoo Keepers" take you the "Very Important Party Animals" on a drinking safari through Key West. Great fun way to get to know your way around the Key West bar scene. Drink like a local, many say it's the best pub crawl in Key West. You get 5 drinks and a t-shirt with our slogan "A Blind Chimp Could Find a Bar on Duval" $35.

Sleeping

Angelina Guesthouse, 302 Angela St, (305) 294-4480, checkout: 11. Clean rooms, shared and private baths, pool, complimentary breakfast, wi-fi. Friendly and helpful staff knowledgeable of the city. $94+.

Atlantis House, 1401 Atlantic Blvd (*1 block from the White Street Pier*), 305-292-1532, checkin: 2PM; checkout: 11AM. 40yds from the Atlantic Ocean and Rest Beach. Beautiful landscaping with only 2 private Jacuzzi Suites. Perfect for Honeymooners and special occasions. Complimentary Wi-Fi, off-street parking and bikes. $149-$275.

Old Town Manor, 511 Eaton Street, 305-292-2170, checkin: 3 PM; checkout: 12 PM. Pet friendly luxury inn located a half block from the excitement of Duval Street. Eco-friendly bed and breakfast with 14 rooms and continental breakfast served daily in our garden courtyard. $115-$375.

Casablanca Bed and Breakfast (*Bogarts Irish Pub*), 900-904 Duval Street, 305-296-0815, Family run bed and breakfast located right on Duval Street just steps away from Old Town. Swimming pool and restaurant/bar located on the premises. Each room has its own private porch and private bathroom. Family friendly.

La Concha Hotel, 430 Duval St, 305-296-2991, Built in 1926 and home of Top Spa on Duval.

Curry Mansion Inn, 511 Caroline Street, +1 800-253-3466, A small hotel just steps from Duval on Caroline, plenty of free parking, open bar cocktail party with piano player every afternoon, breakfast buffet with cooked to order eggs.

Doubletree Grand Key Resort, 3990 South Roosevelt Blvd., 1-888-844-0454 (*dkeyresort.com*), The newest resort-style property among luxury Key West hotels. This place has a good roof top view of the water. For those of you traveling to Key West for poker run and boat races this is a very popular place. However, book early there is limited space available.

Douglas House, 419 Amelia Street, +1 305 294-5269 (). This hotel offers the perfect pool-side setting with swimming pool and heated jacuzzi all surrounded by lush tropical gardens.

Eden House, 1015 Fleming St. (*In Old Town*), +1 305-296-6868, Key West's original guest house. Fully renovated, lush grounds.

Garden House Inn, 329 Elizabeth Street (*parking across st. at church for $10/day*), +1-800-695-6453, checkin: 3PM; checkout: 11AM. A fun and relaxed B&B, with 10 rooms, all with private baths. Amenities include a heated lagoon style pool with spa jets and a cascading waterfall, surrounded by tropical gardens that weave throughout the Inn grounds. Along with a nightly happy hour, a continental breakfast is available each morning. $149 - 299.

Grand Guesthouse Bed and Breakfast, 1116 Grinnell St., +1 888-947-2630 or +1 305-294-0590, In Old Town just a five-block walk from Duval Street and the beach.

Key West City, Florida USA

<u>Heron House Bed & Breakfast</u>, 512 Simonton Street, *+1 305* 294-9227, +1 888 861-9066. . In the heart of the historic district, 23 room bed and breakfast. Complimentary breakfast is served in the mornings and a wine and cheese tasting each night.

<u>Hyatt Key West Resort and Spa</u>, 601 Front Street (*One block from Duval Street*), Newly renovated. Intimate resort with casually elegant Floridian touches, combined with sumptuous, rich fabrics and stunning ocean views. Private marina to fish, scuba, snorkel, parasail, waverunners, or sail on the "Floridays," the resort's 60-foot Irwin sailboat which offers daily sunset cruises and private charter trips. Exercise studio, private beach, pool with oversized whirlpool. Indoor and outdoor dining is available at two restaurants, where guests can watch the sunset.

<u>Island City House Hotel</u>, 411 William Street, +1 305 294-5702, Charming and historical hotel offering 24 suites for lodging near Old Town.

Key West Bed and Breakfast, 415 William Street, +1 800-438-6155, Classic Caribbean Casual. This three story Victorian in the heart of old town is full of color and art.

Pier House Resort and Caribbean Spa, One Duval Street (*On the corner of Duval and the Gulf of Mexico*), 800-327-8340 305-296-4600, checkin: 12:00; checkout: 11:00. Pier House completed an 11 million dollar renovation in 2008. Elegant accommodations, lush gardens, a private beach, a selection of restaurants and bars, a full-service spa.

Reach Resort, 1435 Simonton Street (*in Old Town*), +1 305 296-5000, Spa: +1 305 296-3535, Reservations: +1 888-318-4316, checkin: 4:00 PM; checkout: 11:00 AM. With the only natural beach on the island as a backyard, this hotel is just a block away from Duval Street.

Rose Lane Villas, 511 Eaton Street, 305-292-2170, Pet and family friendly 1,2 & 3 bedroom villas on a quiet street only steps to the heart of Old Town Key West. Swimming pool, parking, fully equipped kitchens and more. $229-$959.

Southern Cross Hotel, 326 Duval Street, 1-888-364-3200, A no-frills hotel with a great location. Located right on Duval Street between Eaton and Caroline. Just steps from everything that Key West has to offer.

Southernmost Hotel, 1319 Duval St, (305) 296-6577, Across the street from the southernmost beach.

Casa Marina Resort, 1500 Reynolds Street, +1 305 296-3535 Reservations: 888-303-5717, checkin: 4:00 PM; checkout: 11:00 AM. A sophisticated Key West resort featuring top-notch dining and pristine private beach.

The Inn at Key West, 3420 N. Roosevelt Blvd. (US 1), Luxury rooms and world-class amenities, accommodations feature a king or double queen size beds some with oversized bathrooms. Freshwater pool, tiki bar and poolside restaurant. Located on the east end of the island, about 3 miles from Duval Street, so it's very quiet and good for families, but you'll need your own car to get to where most of the action is.

Tropical Inn Key West Historic Key West bed and breakfast with Bahamian-style Conch houses. Located on Duval Street.

Historic Key West Inns, 725 Truman Avenue, 305.294.5229, Visitors to Key West, FL will find beauty, warmth and comfort in any of the six hotels that comprise the Historic Key West Inns. All hotels are centrally located in Old Town and provide easy access to the culture and vibe that is Key West. Online reservations available.

Cypress House (*Historic Key West Inns*), 601 Caroline Street (*US 1 to Old Town to Simonton St. Turn right and proceed 8 blocks*), 305.294.6969, Designed for adult couples, guests will find well-appointed, unique and modern rooms in this historical Key West landmark. Start each day with a complimentary, poolside breakfast and then return from the day's revelry to an afternoon mix-n-mingle. Reserve a room at this lush, tropical, gated paradise online today

Key Lime Inn (*Historic Key West Inns*), 305.294.5229, Settle into the fully updated guestrooms spread out across an acre of grounds and experience the property's tranquil, spacious feel. Then step out and walk or pedal to the restaurants and nightlife that is Duval Street. Modern amenities await your arrival. Reserve one of the 37 guestrooms online now

Albury Court (*Historic Key West* Inns), 1030 Eaton Street, Couples looking for romance or planning a Key West honeymoon will delight in the modern amenities, comforts and privacy of this historic hotel. Located in a residential neighborhood, guests can walk to all the area's major attractions. Or perhaps you'll decide to while away the days at our courtyard pool complete with 6 foot waterfall. Check availability and book online

Chelsea House (*Historic Key West Inns*), 709 Truman Avenue, 305.296.2211, Couples with 4 legged family members will enjoy knowing there are a few guestrooms that are pet friendly. Regardless, our guests will enjoy plenty of space to lounge, enjoy the pool and the tropical Victorian architecture. Choose the room with amenities to fit your needs and reserve online today.

Lighthouse Court (*Historic Key West Inns*), 902 Whitehead Street, 305.294.9588, Located near museums, Duval Street and many area favorites, guests will enjoy a wide range of guestrooms and suites. Forty guestrooms throughout ten buildings ensure you'll find the amenities you're looking for from the budget conscious to those seeking luxurious accommodations. Reservations are available online.

Merlin Guesthouse (*Historic Key West Inns*), 811 Simonton Street, 305.296.3336, Families will find rustic modern lodging in a classic guesthouse providing access to all the best of Duval Street and the area beaches. Five buildings in a gated compound surround a private courtyard and pool. A variety of rates helps guests on any budget determine the best style of accommoadations. Book online today.

Historic Key West Inns (Albury Court Hotel), 1030 Eaton Street (At the corner of Frances and Eaton Streets. US 1 bear right at Key West and continue to Old Town about 3 miles), 305.294.5229, One of six Historic Key West Hotels on the island of Key West, Fla. Uniquely styled in the heart of Old Town. Guestrooms offer casual elegance in a historic building. Check availability and reserve online today.

Vacation Homes of Key West (*VHKW*), 507 Whitehead St Key West (*Across from court house on Whitehead St.*), (305) 294-7358, checkin: 4:00pm; checkout: 11:00am. Vacation Homes of Key West ~ key west rentals offered by an established locally operated rental agency representing authentic Old Town villas, cottages, estates, and penthouses for rent in Key West.

Daily, weekly, & monthly rentals available in 1-12 bedroom rental properties. $110-450.

Eden House, 1015 Fleming Street (Florida A1A Key West, FL 33040 Take N Roosevelt Blvd to Palm Avenue Causeway 2.9 mi / 7 min Follow Palm Avenue Causeway, Palm Ave and Eaton St to Fleming St 1.1 mi / 3 min Turn right onto Palm Avenue Causeway 0.4 mi Continue onto Palm Ave 0.3 mi Slight left onto Eaton St 0.2 mi Take the 3rd left onto Grinnell St 390 ft Take the 2nd left onto Fleming St Destination will be on the left), 1-800-533-5397, checkin: 3:00 PM; checkout: 11:00 AM. A tranquil, peaceful setting with all the amenities and none of the attitude. In historic old town Key West, just a short walk from Duval Street.

Eden House hotel offers affordable rates, a heated pool, Jacuzzi, elevated sundeck, waterfalls, hammocks, swings, garden cafe, wi-fi internet service and friendly service - all in a lush, tropical setting. The Eden House is Key West, Florida's original hotel. Built back in 1924, the hotel has been owned and operated since 1975 by

Mike Eden. Now fully renovated and a Green, Eco-Friendly Lodging, the original art deco hotel building is joined by several renovated conch houses, making for a lovely property with a full range of accommodations - from apartment suites to semi-private rooms, and everything in between.

The Marker Resort Key West, 200 William Street, 855-969-3206, A luxury waterfront resort on the Historic Seaport of Key West offering spacious accommodations, complimentary Wi-Fi, complimentary parking, three tropical tree-lined pools and more.

Key West Realty, 1121 Duval St., Key West, FL 33040, 305-292-6266, Last Key Realty is a vacation rental broker and buyer's broker in Key West, Florida offering the most meticulously furnished and maintained vacation rental properties in Key West.

Ocean's Edge Key West, 5950 Peninsular Avenue, Key West FL 33040, 305-809-8204, Located in Key West's

Stock Island neighborhood, Ocean's Edge Key West features acres of deep-water access, an onsite marina, onsite access to fishing charters and six oceanfront pools. Family built, run and operated, the resort offers oceanfront rooms and suites with floor-to-ceiling windows boasting a full ocean view and a private balcony. Ocean's Edge also features seafood dining at Yellowfin Bar & Grill.

Camping

There is no longer any camping in Key West, but you can still find some just outside the City limits on Stock Island. Within Key West itself, parking is very limited and RV's are generally discouraged, so your best shot is to stay somewhere outside the city and drive a smaller vehicle into town.

Boyds Key West Campground, 6401 Maloney Ave., +1 305 294-1465 . Boyd's is a family owned and operated campground and RV park that opened in 1963. Only 5 miles from Duval Street and downtown (3 miles to Smathers Beach) and has city bus and taxi service to all of Key West. Oceanfront and able to accommodate the largest RVs as well as tent camping with marina space for your boat. It has a pool, laundry, gameroom, boutique, 4 bathhouses and nighttime security.

El Mar RV Resort, 6700 Maloney Ave., *+1 305* 294-0857

Leo's Campground & RV Park, 5236 Suncrest Rd., *+1 305* 296-5260,

There are a few more a little ways up the Keys that cater to RVs. The number of campsites are limited, so do not be shocked by the price. Make your reservations well in advance six months to a year so you are sure to get your spot. You will notice the use of "MM" or "Mile Marker" in the addresses. This is how US 1 is marked. MM 0 is in Old town Key West and the beginning of US 1. The numbers go up, so you can tell just how far an address is from Key West.

- ✓ Bluewater Key - Clark's RV Lot Rentals, Mile Marker 14.3, Sugarloaf, +1 305 744-0999 .

- ✓ Bluewater Key RV Resort, MM 14.3 U.S. 1 Sugarloaf Key, +1 305 745-2494,
- ✓ Geiger Key Marina and RV Park, 5 Geiger Road, Big Coppitt Key, +1 305 296-3553,
- ✓ Sugarloaf Key Resort KOA Kampground, MM 20 Summerland Key, +1 305 745-3549 (800) 562-7731,

Cope

Key West is well known as a gay tourism mecca, so if homosexuality offends you consider giving Key West a miss. Having said that, however, the LGBT community (both tourist and resident) adds a great deal of fun, colour and livelihood to Key West and if you have an open mind then it becomes an important and enriching part of the Key West experience.

Stay Safe

Violent crime is extremely rare, but vehicle break-ins and pick-pocketing are not uncommon. Key West is home to a large homeless population. Most are harmless, but many suffer from drug and/or alcohol addiction and resort to aggressive panhandling and petty crime to finance their addictions. Use the same level of common sense you would use elsewhere in the USA...keep valuables out of plain view, park your vehicle in a well-lit, heavy traffic area and if you get lost try not to make it too obvious.

Pay attention to the weather. The Keys are a narrow band of islands that offer little protection from tropical storms. In the past storms have generated waves with enough strength to demolish bridges and topple freight trains and engines sitting on tracks. The locals seem immune to these dangers: rely on National Weather reports, rather than the opinion of locals. If it is suggested you go back to the mainland, do so immediately. There is one highway in and out. The Overseas Highway can and will be closed for a period should a car or truck accident occur. Always allow extra time if traveling back to the mainland to meet a flight or cruise.

Key West is well known as a popular tourism location for the LGBT community. The LGBT community (both tourist and resident) in Key West is open and vibrant and adds a great deal of fun, color and livelihood to Key West.

Vacation Rental Availability
By The Beautiful Sea

If you're craving a Key West beach accommodation with a bone fide front-line view to the sea, you know they're not easy to come by. But in this pretty vacation rental condominium, *By The Beautiful Sea*, you can instantly gratify this need for sensational vistas from your own vacation rental terrace right across the street from the beach. Make your first order of the day to breathe in the fresh ocean breezes with a walk along the beach and fulfill the desire to dig those toes into warm white sand . . . for after all your front yard *is* the

Atlantic Ocean. Your 'back yard' view is not bad either. The entrance for this property connects with a second level walkway of the building, and offers views of beautiful tropical park-like landscaping. A short stroll from the condominium through the landscaped setting, leads to the large free form swimming pool and Jacuzzi. A major decision each day could be whether to enjoy the sun at the beach or pool side. And when it's time to go dining, shopping, or enjoying the nightlife, Old Town is close by and an easy bike ride away. Ahhhh . . . life in paradise is good.

The interior layout of this property was designed to maximize the opportunity to take in the ocean view from the living room and dining area, as well as the master bedroom. Sliding glass doors off the living room, lead to a private ocean view terrace. The kitchen adjoins the dining room through a pass through door, creating a floor plan that makes it easy for entertaining the family or a group of friends.

The layout of the bedrooms is ideal for a family or three couples. You'll need to flip a coin for the enviable master suite that has the ocean view, plus a door that leads directly to the sea-side balcony. Furnishings are tropical elegant with a honey-colored wood-and-wicker king size bed and romantic free-standing grandfather clock to remind you that it's 5 o'clock somewhere. Another nice feature of the master bedroom is a walk-in closet. Next to this closet, the master bath provides a long vanity with two sinks, tiled floor, and bath-tub with in-tub shower.

The other two bedrooms and second bathroom, are on the opposite side of the condominium, down a short hallway, just off the great-room. Immediately off the hall to the right is a bedroom with two twin beds, which can be made up as a king size bed upon request. Nicely decorated with white cottage furnishings, there is also plenty of daylight that streams in through a nice size window. Directly at the end of the hallway is the third bedroom with king size bed. Handsome honey-colored wooden furnishings fill the room in nice contrast with the coral colored walls. A window on one wall invites in the natural light.

The second full bathroom, with standing shower and glass door, is situated off the hallway, easily accessed by both the second and third bedrooms. This bathroom also conveniently houses the washer/dryer, a welcome feature for a beach house, where you can come in and drop your towels and wet bathing suits.

A notable layout feature of this property is that it's an end unit in the condominium building, making it one of the more desirable locations in the complex as you only have neighbors on one side. It is located on the first floor, but elevated second level, since the covered parking is directly below. This design provides a wonderful view of the ocean. The entrance to the unit can be reached by stairs or elevator. There is designated covered parking, and the condominium complex is gated and secured with an electronic key entrance.

Bedding Summary:

- ➢ Master Bedroom 1 King size bed
- ➢ Bedroom 2 2 Twin Beds (can be made as a king size bed)
- ➢ Bedroom 3 King size bed

Amenities: Located in a beach condominium complex across the street from Key West Smathers' Beach. Private balcony with front-line view to the sea. Balcony access from great-room and master suite. Resort style heated swimming pool, hot tub, separate men and women saunas and changing rooms near pool for guest use only. Tennis courts, propane BBQ grills on the grounds. Fully equipped kitchen, central A/C, Wi-Fi, cable TV and DVD, stereo, washer / dryer. Linens and towels are provided. Maid service can be scheduled.

Activities: Everything beach! Sunning, swimming, catamaran rentals, volleyball, beach food trucks. Easy walk to the White Street Pier, Salute Restaurant for dining on the beach, ocean front children's playground, historic garden club, nature preserve, much more. A bike / walking path winds along the ocean and leads you to the heart of Old Town Key West where you find restaurants, nightlife, museums, everything Key West has to offer.

Area: This area of Key West is often referred to as the beachside neighborhood due to the close proximity to the southern shore of the island. This part of the island feels like a beach town neighborhood with light ocean breezes, and it's not unusual to see folks walking or biking on the bike path in their bathing suits with towel and cooler under arm. A paved biking and walking path stretches along the southern shore dotted with parks and food and water sport concessions making it easy and interesting to stroll or bike. There is a pre-Civil War Fort along the waterfront, West Martello near Higgs Beach that now houses the Key West Garden Club.

Parking: Designated covered parking for one vehicle. One additional vehicle may park in the adjoining lot. All vehicles parked must display parking passes issued by the condominium. Scooter parking allowed. Bicycle racks near elevator. No boats, RV's, Jet ski's or trailers of any kind are allowed in the parking area.

Restrictions: No smoking. This condominium is offered as a vacation rental in a preferred beachfront condominium in Key West. Pets are not allowed. We do not accept guests less than 25 years of age unless accompanied by a family group or guardian. No boat, trailer (bike or boat), jet ski, or RV parking. Guests must agree to abide by condominium regulations.

Villa Nouveau Key West

Sometimes a Key West cottage that at first glance appears predictable from the outside, is full of abundant surprises when you walk inside. *Villa Nouveau Key West* vacation rental has an interesting story that attests to this truth. Once a prosaic 'shotgun' style cottage, a modern redesign has thoughtfully transformed it into a sophisticated 'L-Shape' 4 bedroom 4 bathroom pool-side courtyard villa. An ambitious and creative change, this fabulous property was recently renovated to receive a luxury pool-side great room, 4 beautiful bedrooms, and a custom designed private swimming pool and lounging deck.

Interior: The interior décor draws from a soft tropical color palate of blues and sand tones and incorporates elegant modern furnishings of leather and wood. Floors throughout are tiled with earth tone travertine marble. Architectural angles and recessed lighting make the spaces fresh and spacious. An open concept kitchen-dining room-living room is finished with modern wooden cabinets, granite counter tops, upscale appliances and fixtures, and boasts a state-of-the-art entertainment center with a large screen TV placed over a wet-bar.

For sleeping, the bedrooms shown on the graphic as number 1, 2 and 3 provide king size beds (#1 is a California King), while bedroom number 4 provides 1 full and one twin beds. Each of the 4 bedrooms provides a private en-suite bathroom. Bedrooms with king size beds provide spacious walk-in showers, while the bedroom with the twin and full beds offers a bath tub with in-tub shower.

Grounds: The Villa Nouveau vacation rental is situated at the southeast corner and the rear of the grounds Grande Dame Key West The Watson House estate. It is made private with tall wooden privacy walls between the properties and a separate entrance on the extreme south side of the grounds just beyond the parking area. The villa has a beautiful 'L- Shape' private pool set into the back deck. It follows the line of the house, and curves around the corner of the house outside the great-room and is visible and accessible through three sets of single-pane French doors.

Designed to comfortably sleep 8, if your group grows, it's possible to rent this home in combination with the larger estate home, the <u>Grande Dame Key West 'The Watson House</u>,' next door. When rented in its entirety, it is offered as an exclusive vacation rental compound we call, The Meeting Point Key West. If you are looking to accommodate a larger group, renting the 4 bedroom villa and 7 bedroom main estate home provides one of the most unique and beautiful private vacation rental properties in Key West.

Bedding Summary:

2 King size beds, 1 California King size bed, 1 Full and 1 Twin size beds

Amenities: New construction, upscale renovation. Private swimming pool, private deck off great-room. Fully equipped kitchen, central a/c, color cable TV, stereo, washer / dryer. Linens and towels are provided. Off street parking for 1 car. Catering can be arranged. Maid service can be scheduled.

Activities: Heart of Key West's designated historic district from here you can walk to all Old Town features. Enjoy the pedestrian life-style and walk everywhere with no need for a car. One short street and one minute walk from the 500 block of Duval St. Close to Mallory Square, and a few short streets from

Historic Seaport and retailers. Sailing, boating, diving, museums, nightlife, family activities. Conveniently located to gourmet grocery shopping with excellent wine selection, sushi deli, and butcher. Close to shopping, art galleries, and a variety of national and international restaurants, coffee shops. Close to the beach.

Area: On Simonton Street, a famous residential street in the tiny section of Key West that is the "island urban" area. A beautiful stand of grand residential homes are in this area. When you stay in this tiny district it's amazing how much there is to see. One street from the mid-point of Duval Street in Old Town Key West that grew up as the central downtown area in the late 1800's.

Restrictions: While this property is ideal for families and groups to unite, it is not suitable for staging loud parties. Smoking permitted outside only. Absolutely no pets. Please don't ask. We do not accept guests less than 25 years of age unless accompanied by a family group or guardian.

Villa Deja vu Key West

You know that incredible experience of Déjà vu? When you enter someplace for the very first time, and instantly you get that sense that you've been there before? When I first visited this vacation rental house, it happened to me. My mind sparked, the place seemed wonderfully familiar, and I felt an instant kinship with the surroundings.

As I toured the house and the grounds of the property, I quickly realized that my brain was just catching up to my fondest memories of favorite beach vacations in other parts of the Caribbean. The creative blend of tropical color and playfully elegant style reminded me of a favorite vacation villa in St. Barth's and an endearing beach house in The Bahamas. A carefree beachiness permeates every room of this two-story wooden house and it had taken me right back to bliss.

After that moment of recall it was then pronounced the **Villa Déjà vu Key West**. *

Ideally located, this property is set at the end of a quiet historic 'dead end' lane, just off the more elegant area of Upper Duval Street, in Old Town. Each house on the little lane is completely unique, mostly 'build-as-you-go' creations of skilled ship builders and carpenters in the 1940's. This historic wooden house, originally built in 1943 has an uncharacteristically unornamented front entrance for Key West, and is set right up to the edge of the lane. But don't let this illusion of simplicity fool you. Most of the outdoor space is reserved for the very spacious private backyard, which today has been turned into a showcase tropical pool garden.

The entire property was recently given a complete renovation and new interior design to bring it to modern standards. But in keeping with Key West historic guidelines, the footprint and façade of the house remain in tact. The layout of the Villa Déjà vu Key West vacation rental is ideal for family groups or groups of friends. The floor plan provides 2 spacious separate floors which are adjoined with a covered indoor/outdoor staircase, with a large indoor living room, and pool garden with large deck for all to gather. The 2nd floor is set so it almost feels like two houses in one.

Interior Layout:

Since the unique layout of this property is anything but straight-forward, the best way to understand it is to do a virtual walk-through. What better place to begin our tour, than the front entrance.

The front door takes you directly into an outdoor tropical style entrance hall, where you find the usual expected accoutrements of a chair and mirror for last minute fussing. (Immediately to your right, is a door that leads to the master bedroom, but let's leave that late for later when we look at that bedroom.)

From the entrance way a door takes you into the downstairs hallway. When I first stepped into the hall, I was awestruck by the floor-to-ceiling mural depicting a Key West lane, painted by locally famous artist Rick Worth. The next thing you'll notice is the artistic wide-planked wood floor that was distressed and painted a wonderful Caribbean blue that leads straight ahead to the large, and very island-stylish, galley kitchen.

Kitchen: The fully equipped L-Shaped kitchen spans nearly the length of the house, and makes a bend toward the left at the end creating even more counter space. Lots of artistic touches make this a fun room to be in. I love the counter-height cottage style table and yellow art mural of a vintage Cuban menu board. A bank of sash windows is set above the counters at the back to bring in plenty of sunlight.

Bedroom / Bathroom One: With your back to the front entrance, looking toward the kitchen, the first door on your left is bedroom one. Here you'll find a queen size bed with artistic handcrafted furnishings including wooden bed platform bed, lime-green headboard, and unique round bamboo end tables. Original distressed wide-planked floors are left a natural color in this room.

The bathroom for this bedroom is just out the door, a few steps past the cottage-style kitchen table to your left. The bathroom is decorated with Caribbean island theme art and offers a full shower, and was recently refitted with an apron front sink and dark-wood vanity.

Living Room: The sunken' living room is on the opposite of the hallway from the first bedroom and bathroom. Spacious, artful and colorful all the way, there are too many special touches to mention. Bright and cushy canvas furnishings set against the wide-planked wooden floors and a reclaimed wooden Key West Navy trunk create relaxed island feel. A large white handcrafted 'picnic-style' dining table, lit with a pretty chandelier, is placed overlooking the pool garden. A large wide screen TV is hung on the wall towards the kitchen in case you need it. A vintage 'Discovery Undersea Tours' sign is featured as a show piece on the opposite wall from the TV.

Master Bedroom Suite: The master bedroom suite includes a sitting room / office, bedroom, and en-suite bathroom. The sitting room adjoins the left side of the living room, as you face the kitchen. In the photograph, you see the wicker chaise painted a coral color, and the corner of the writing desk painted a white patina.

Straight ahead, is the master bedroom with a queen size bed using similar artistic handcrafted furnishings as bedroom one, including a wooden platform bed. This time the artsy headboard is made with reclaimed shutters that are painted white patina along with the end tables. An added feature is the doorway that leads to the entrance hall, and the stairs that lead to the 2nd floor. Wood floors are left a natural color in the entire suite, except for the bathroom which has earth-tone tile. The master bathroom, which adjoins the sitting room, is shown with the antique wall mirror adorned with a starfish.

Second Floor Bedrooms and Bathroom: A hidden switch-back staircase off the downstairs entrance way, leads up to the 2nd floor bedrooms via a private entrance. A covered sitting porch, with classic Key West gingerbread railings, spans nearly the entire width of the 2nd floor of the house. Nestled behind mature tropical trees, the porch provides an exotic outdoor space with a private down look view of the lane below.

Step inside to a beautiful tropical 2nd floor suite with dark hard wood floors. Painted in white, and styled in soft colors, the 3rd bedroom is furnished with a queen sized bed and built in closet.

The 4th bedroom, which also provides a queen size bed, is located behind a white louvered wall at the back corner of the 2nd floor. White wicker and white patina framed mirrors in this bedroom make a striking contrast with the dark wood floors. The full bathroom for the 2nd floor carries the tropical white wicker on white theme. It provides a vanity with marble top, tiled floor, and a shower.

Pool Garden Grounds:

The spacious private back yard with swimming pool, sun deck, and lush landscaping is focal point of Villa Déjà vu Key West. Access this space through a double set of French doors topped with wide transom windows, just off the living room. A large blue awning covers the deck and is set as an outdoor living room with nice wood furnishings. A playful sign over the couch sets the tone, "Welcome To The Beach." Even though you're not right on the beach, South Beach is just a few short streets up Duval Street, but with this kind of privacy you just might end up spending most of your time right here. A combination of high fencing lined with an impressive variety of tall mature palm trees surround the decked courtyard and make a private backdrop for the nice size swimming pool with trickling waterfall.

Laundry: There is a laundry closet with a washer / dryer on the pool deck, on the back wall of the house near the kitchen.

The general design of this property lends itself perfectly to small gatherings of families and friends and should be considered an ideal spot for a gathering of family or friends.

Note: This is a private vacation rental villa, not to be confused with the former Déjà vu Resort in Key West that was closed in 2008.

Bedding Summary:

- Bedroom #1 - 1st floor 1 queen size bed
- Bedroom #2 - 1st floor Master suite 1 queen size bed.
- Bedroom #3 - 2nd floor 1 queen size bed
- Bedroom #4 - 2nd floor 1 queen size bed

Amenities: Tucked back at the end of a 'dead end' lane hidden from view. Large back yard with private swimming pool, large sun deck, and lush landscaped garden, outdoor covered living room, privacy fences. 2ndfloor porch overlooking lane below. Fully equipped kitchen, a/c, cable TVs, stereo, internet. Laundry room with washer / dryer. Linens and towels are provided. Catering can be arranged. Maid service can be scheduled.

Activities: Elegant Upper Duval St. A few short streets from South Beach, close to the Southern Most Point of the United States. Café pedestrian neighborhood features wonderful eateries and internationally famous fine restaurants, coffee & tea house, fine gift and clothing stores, art galleries Grand Vin wine tasting, home made ice cream and frozen yogurt. Here you start at the top of Duval St. near the Atlantic Ocean and can take the 20 min stroll to the Gulf of Mexico (remember it takes 3 to 4 Key West streets to equal the distance of a typical city block). Sailing, boating, diving, museums, nightlife.

Area: Elegant Upper Duval Street neighborhood. Walk out your door and down the lane to all you want to see in Historic Key West. Historic area originally built around the Gato Cigar Factory in the 19th century. Lane where this house is located features a unique one-of-a-king collection of hand crafted historic wooden homes. Close to best restaurants, clubs, Hemingway House Museum, Light House Museum, Custom House Museum, aquarium, Ship Wreck Museum. Walk or bike to all Old Town features from here.

Restrictions: Smoke free house. No pets! (Please don't ask). We do not accept guests less than 25 years of age unless accompanied by a family group or guardian.

Caribbean Cottage

Imagine the quintessential Caribbean island village, its cottages nestled hand-in-hand on charming historic pedestrian streets. As people stroll by, sun kissed from an afternoon of beaching and sight seeing, they'll say hi to one another even if they've never met. This is your neighborhood during your stay at the *Caribbean Cottage*vacation rental. One of the best vacation rental locations on the island - without a doubt. Around the corner "Grand Vin" wine bar stands ready for an evening wine tasting session while "Flamingo Crossing" ice cream parlor offers up a new flavor of home made glace.

Brimming with genuine island charm, our Caribbean Cottage, with private pool, was originally built in the early 1900's. Artistically renovated to maintain the original wood planked polished floors and vintage hand-hewed beams, the owners added bright blue tile (accented with marble), and Bahama style wooden window shutters tat compliment the historic interior. Original pine walls were painted with elegant historic colors of olive and cream and adorned the sash style windows and French linen curtains. Reserved for owner's use only for many years, original artwork from their private collection is displayed throughout for you to enjoy.

The living room is a generous cottage size with plenty of room to gather. On the side closest to the kitchen, a dining table is placed to create a roomy eating area. The adjoining "butler-pantry" style kitchen is spacious, has a charming French-Caribbean style ambiance, and is fully equipped and easy to cook in.

The interior lay-out of this cottage maximizes privacy with the bedrooms and bathrooms on one side and common living areas on the other. The cottage has two full bedrooms and two full bathrooms.

Bedding in this vintage cottage includes a king size bed in the master bedroom, and a queen size bed in the other. The master bedroom boasts a beautiful rich wooden armoire, and French doors lead from the bedroom to a pretty outdoor sitting area for reading and lounging. For extra sleeping, the living room has a comfortable twin daybed.

From the outside front, the cottage has charming curb appeal with a large beautiful Royal Poinciana tree and the Key West quintessential white picket fence, and of course the porch to sit and watch the world go by. The general design and layout of the cottage lends itself perfectly for versatile use. It is ideal for up to four, and can sleep up to five people comfortably.

If you are looking for a truly authentic Key West experience, this cottage could be the perfect one for you. This charming property is located in the Upper-Duval Street historic neighborhood - a special section of Key West offering many up-scale attractions and interesting features including excellent gourmet restaurants, art galleries, boutiques, a high-end wine tasting store, an award winning home made ice cream shop, a coffee and tea house, South Beach around the corner, and .just a short walk to down to Mallory Square.

There is off-street parking for one full size car, but from here you really never need to get in your car. Upper Duval Street is right out your front door, so forget the hassle of parking and enjoy walking or biking everywhere. Enjoy the island to the fullest, and then come home to relax in the pool.

Key West City, Florida USA

Bedding Summary:

- ➢ Master bedroom - King size bed
- ➢ 2nd Bedroom- Queen size bed
- ➢ Living Room - Twin daybed

Amenities: Champagne for the newly weds! Private pool with bricked courtyard garden, fenced yard, fully equipped kitchen. A/C, washer / dryer, Flat screen color cable TV, C/D player and stereo, wireless internet. Linens and towels are provided.

Activities: Shopping, restaurants, nightlife, museums, sailing, boating, snorkeling, diving, theatre, night life, family activities. Everything is within walking distance. Cafe neighborhood features art galleries, wonderful eateries and internationally famous fine restaurants, coffee house, fine gift and clothing stores. Right out your gate find Grand Vin Wine Bar, where you'll enjoy a broad selection of wine by the glass and Flamingo Crossing, *the award winning homemade ice cream store with some of the best ice cream you'll ever eat.*

Key West South Beach is a 3 minute walk up the street at most Upper end of Duval St.

Area: Upper Duval or 'Uptown Key West' has evolved into the "elegant end of Duval" and offers an exceptional variety of restaurants, beautiful boutiques, and art galleries. Walk to South Beach in 3 minutes and the Southernmost Point of the United States is just down the street and around the corner. Walk to the Mallory Square Sunset Celebration in 15 to 20 minutes.

Parking: Off-street parking for one car.

Restrictions: Smoke free house. No Pets. We do not accept guests less than 25 years of age unless accompanied by a family group or guardian.

Note: If you love this cottage but need to sleep more than 4 in beds, you can rent it with the one bedroom Vintage Luxury Cottage. You can combine a rental of both cottages and sleep 8 by renting the Fantasy Resort Villa. When rented together, you have two private swimming pools.

Key West City, Florida USA

Key West Wabi Sabi

Undeniably adorable, Key West Wabi Sabi vacation rental is a celebration of authentic Key West cottage style island living. Built in 1930, the front of the historic wooden plank house is held to vintage form with loads of original details, complete with welcoming front porch and saw-tooth tin roof. True to its name, the interior was lovingly redesigned to time-honor its nostalgic charm and simplicity and is beautifully renovated with luxury conveniences and amenities that complement the style. Enjoy our architectural photographs of each room and the back deck plus a detailed floor plan of the interior.

About the Design:

What's in a name? Wabi Sabi is often summarized as "the wisdom of simplicity" and finding the "natural beauty in imperfection. From an aesthetic standpoint, Old Town Key West, full of history nostalgia is an architectural reflection of this notion. It was this concept that inspired the make-over of this precious vintage house.

The owners love the aesthetic of Old Town Key West architecture and wanted to retain the vintage heritage of this house while at the same time making a vacation home that is light, airy, cozy, peaceful and relaxing. Committed to the life concepts of authenticity and sustainability, they traveled to vintage markets in northern California to hand-select a wonderful collection of one-of-a-kind repurposed furnishings scaled to the size of the home. Period pieces were chosen for their curvy vintage lines and surfaces painted soft pastels and whites. A variety of wooden furniture styles and unique artwork are beautifully blended with unique lighting fixtures to complement one another to create a romantic shabby chic style. A touch of rich reds and bright greens and turquoise add a Key West tropical punch. The end result is a space where you can slow down, take a break from this crazy-mixed -up world, and recharge your batteries - island style.

Interior Layout: Sweet and sensuous, the alluring spaces of this delightful vintage cottage style house speak to the heart. Because it's a tropical home, the floor plan has been re-worked to focus the main living area toward the back yard so that indoor / outdoor pool-side living is maximized. In this re-design, the front of the house became bedrooms. The living room is now accessed through a side entrance situated on the left side of the house from the private driveway. Step into the entrance hall and you're faced with a door to your left leading to the living / dining / kitchen area, a stairway straight ahead that leads to the 2nd floor master suite, and a door to your right that leads to the 3rd and 4th bedrooms. Refer to the slide show of the first floor and we will begin our tour of the house at the back main living area.

Living room / dining room / kitchen:

Designed as an open concept great-room with double sets of single pane French doors that lead to the pool and wooden deck, this is the common living area where you will gather to visit, relax and dine together. Thick Mexican tiled floors and soaring open beamed ceiling painted white punctuate the cottage style and create an open spacious feeling. A beautiful hand hewed round white wooden dining table and chairs is set near the doors for garden view dining. A vintage style living room grouping of sofa, period piece chairs, occasional tables and lamps is set on the wall facing the back deck. A cottage-style custom kitchen with all the modern conveniences runs along the entire north wall.

Bedrooms:

The house provides 4 bedrooms, 3 which can be considered 'master bedrooms' since they provide full en-suite bathrooms. The 4th bedroom doubles as a den and offers a powder room (1/2 bath) with sink and commode. Refer to our slide show to clarify the layout of the bedrooms as described below.

Bedroom 1 - The 1st bedroom, with en-suite bath, is accessed through a door between the living room and kitchen. This bedroom has the same soaring open beam ceilings as the great-room, and with two sash windows that let in plenty of sunlight it feels airy and spacious. This bedroom is staged with a craftsman built wooden king size platform bed. A hand painted headboard and beautiful 'Beach House' sign perched above the door, combined with a combination of vintage and tropical furnishings create a special welcoming island feel. The full bathroom provides a tub, tiled in-tub shower, and free-standing sink.

Bedroom 2 - Refer to the graphic in our slide show of the 2nd floor to begin our tour of the 2nd bedroom with private en-suite bathroom. Accessed from the wooden interior staircase, this is the only room on the 2nd floor. This room is ½ story, so the front half of the ceiling has a low slant. A non-issue only to be noted, there is plenty of head room to stand up straight and walk around in the rest of the space.

Considered the main master bedroom in the house, a little romance sets the tone for this 2nd floor story-book suite. Distressed wide wood planked floors with custom cut nails, and a little private balcony harken the authentic tone of the room. A queen size wooden platform bed painted white is neatly tucked in the dormered sleeping alcove on one side of the room. An adorable 1940's vanity and re-claimed designer slipper chair with ottoman are set on the other side and curtains matching the peacock pattern chair and ottoman complete the decorator look. The vintage style bathroom, complete with claw-foot bathtub with in-tub shower, is pretty and peaceful.

Bedroom 3 - Located at the front of the house, on the left side as you face it, the 3rd bedroom is accessed from the main side entrance of the house. Designed to be used as a bedroom or a den, this room has received a total renovation by ripping out the old tile floors and ugly ceiling and adding fresh new cottage-style cypress wood planked floors a bead board ceiling. Three sash windows at the side and front of the house are kept in tack to invite in the natural daylight.

This is the smallest of the 3 bedrooms, but it is comfortably furnished with a trundle bed that can be made up as 2 twin beds or a king size bed. A charming vintage wood dresser, end tables and chair complete the dressed-down charming feel. This room provides a pretty cottage style powder room (1/2 bath) complete with an artistic corner vanity with round pottery sink, matching back-splash tiles, and a pretty little stained glass window set over the sink to invite in light from the entrance hall.

Bedroom 4 - Situated at the front of the house, on the right side as you face it, the 4th bedroom can be accessed from 2 entrances. Refer to the floor plan to see how an interior door joins bedroom 3 and 4, so these rooms can be opened to use together or separately. But please note, bedroom 4 is also accessed from the front door of the house, giving it a private entrance from the front porch. This gives the added option of using the front door entrance for bedroom 4 so as not to disturb persons using bedroom 3 for sleeping.

In the re-design, the 4th bedroom received the same cypress wood planked floors bead board ceiling as the adjoining bedroom 3. It also enjoys the same style sash windows, only on the opposite side and front of the house. For furnishings, this bedroom provides a king size bed and fabulous period furniture that includes a hand crafted armoire and dresser. This bedroom is completed with an en-suite bathroom with tiled shower, free-standing sink, commode and a vanity shelf nook.

Grounds: One of the nicest features of the property is the indoor / outdoor tropical life-style it provides. Double sets of single pane French doors open from the great room to the back wooden deck. Visible from the main living area, the pretty pool with trickling waterfall is large enough to float around and relax, but like most pools in Key West, don't expect to dive and do laps. The fully fenced deck area provides lounge chairs and an exterior dining chair and tables for poolside snacking.

At the front of the property, the house boasts a whimsical curbside appeal with a saw-tooth tin roof. An irresistible front porch spans the width of the building, with a center door framed by wood shutters and sash hung windows. A Key West signature white picket fence surrounds the front and sides. Simple tropical foliage grows in the small front yard between the fence and the porch. At the left side of the property in the front, is a private off-street parking place for one

Notes: This property works best for 8 people. Bedroom 3 has a ½ only, so you will need to decide which bathroom to shower in. When bedrooms 3 & 4 are used together with the adjoining door, they can work ideally for a couple with a child or 2 children.

Bedding Summary:

- ➢ Bedroom 1 King size bed
- ➢ Bedroom 2 (2nd FL) Queen size bed
- ➢ Bedroom 3 Trundle bed (can be made as 2 twin beds or a king size bed
- ➢ Bedroom 4 King size bed

Amenities: Float pool and deck. New fully equipped kitchen, a/c, Wi-Fi, cable TV and DVD, stereo, washer / dryer. Linens and towels are provided. Catering can be arranged. Maid service can be scheduled.

Parking: Wabi-sabi enthusiasts tend to embrace simplicity in daily life by living in smaller homes, driving smaller cars. Private off - street parking for one compact size car in driveway. DO NOT BRING AN OVERSIZED VEHICLE TO THIS SPACE AS IT WILL NOT FIT. If you arrive by car plan to park it in your designated private parking space and enjoy walking or biking around the island.

Activities: This property is located just a few blocks from Mallory Square Sunset Celebration, steps from Fausto's Fine Foods for grocery shopping, excellent downtown restaurants, popular clubs, the Historic Seaport, and tropical shops makes this one of the most requested and convenient accommodations in Key West.

Area: Downtown Old Town Historic Key West. Just one-half block off Duval Street. Walk to all Old Town Key West features. Great restaurants, shops, galleries, clubs, Hemingway House Museum, Light House Museum, Custom House Museum, Key West Aquarium, Ship Wreck Museum. 10 minute stroll from the famous Sunset Celebration at Mallory Square.

Restrictions: Smoke free house. No pets. This home is offered as an exclusive vacation rental in the most requested location in Key West. We do not accept guests less than 25 years of age unless accompanied by a family group or guardian.

A Tropical Tradition (Gallup Arms)

Nestled in one of Key West's original gated "mini-compounds," the Tropical Tradition vacation rental is a spacious 1990's three-story Key West town home providing an island living experience in a traditional tropical style - both inside and out. A lush tropical garden complete with large 40' X 16' swimming pool is the main focus of this unique island setting, and this traditional Key West town-home home is situated at the "pool-side" of the garden.

The main entrance to this home leads from the front porch to the living room / dining and open U-shaped kitchen which makes meal preparation and entertaining relaxed and fun. French doors and multiple sets of sash windows fill the room with light and high ceilings provide a spacious feeling. Casual Florida style furnishings are traditional tropical bent-wood bamboo and wicker that blend nicely with the light hard wood floors. The first floor also offers the convenience of a powder room (sink and commode) and a door beneath the stairwell conveniently hides the washer / dryer. A traditional banister wooden staircase leads from the living room to the second floor where you find one bedroom with a queen size bed, a full bathroom, and a sitting room that opens to a covered porch through French doors. The porch has a beautiful down-look view of the swimming pool and garden. The staircase continues from the sitting room to the third floor which provides two more bedrooms and a full bathroom.

The floor plan on the third level has the bedrooms on opposite sides with a shared full bath in between. One bedroom offers a queen size bed and the other has 2 twin beds. The second level has one bedroom offering a queen size bed, and opposite the bedroom is a den with balcony overlooking the pool. All bedrooms have nice views of either the pool or a garden area below. Bedroom furnishings carry the traditional Florida tropical wicker and bent bamboo theme established on the first floor. This property is offered as an exclusive vacation rental in Old Town Key West.

The property will not tolerate smoking inside. The property is located in a private residential compound and is definitely not suitable for staging loud parties.

Bedding Summary:

- ➢ Second Floor - 1 queen size bed
- ➢ Third Floor - 1 queen, 2 twin beds

Amenities: Gated "mini compound" with spacious shared lush tropical garden. Large 40' X 16' feet swimming pool (no heat, shared) directly in front of the town-home. Flat-screen cable TV's, central a/c, stereo, telephone, washer dryer, linens and towels provided, fenced yard, first and second floor porches overlooking pool and garden.

Activities: Conveniently located close to grocery shopping, art galleries, French Country and Cuban cuisine, and deli restaurant and bakery. Close to the beach (a short walk), and 2 parks. Ride your bike to

Duval Street and the Southern most point of the U.S. in fewer than five minutes. Walk to Duval Street in 20 minutes..

Area: This town home is ideally located in the White Street Gallery District of Old Town Key West in a historic residential neighborhood just a few streets from White Street and Higgs Beach. From this location you can quickly walk to Fausto's Fine Food Palace (fine wine, cheeses, and gourmet foods), Sandy's Cafe of Cuban coffee, numerous art galleries (White Street Gallery area), and yoga and exercise studios. Duval Street shops, attractions, and the Historic Seaport District is a ten minute walk.

Restrictions: Smoke free house. Sleeps six (6) maximum guests. No pets (please don't ask.) We do not accept guests less than 25 years of age unless accompanied by a family group or guardian.

Notes: If you are planning a vacation get-together and need accommodate a larger group, you can rent one or all of the properties that are part of the Family Reunion vacation rental compound.

Lazy Iguana

This genuine Key West combo of our Private Pool Garden Villa plus a classy private studio cottage that adjoins the property next door, can be your very own get-away for a week or more. When rented together, we call the property the *Lazy Iguana.* Off-the-beaten path of most tourist homes and harkening back to the last bastion of Key West bohemia, the Lazy Iguana vacation rental is a fixture of the remaining literary old guard in Key West. With this property you will enjoy beautiful authenticity that pre-dates the last decade of rapid gentrification on Key West with comfort, style, and privacy.

We invite you to laze-away the hot summer days or unwind your mind in tropical autumn, in the cooling freshness of this genuine Key West tropical pool garden property. While sun sizzles on the white sandy beaches, turquoise waters surrounding the island warm to a luxurious temperature beckoning those who love to spend their down-time in the tropics.

But Key West is famous for its refreshing tropical gardens too, and in the warm seasons lush island flora strike their pose with vibrant orange blooms of flamboyant Poinciana and brilliant climbing red and purple bougainvillea. Fuzzy fragrant pink flowers sprout from exotic mimosa trees and tiny fragrant white stars of night blooming jasmine invite you to retreat to the garden. Take a deep breath, refresh your spirit with a dip the pool, then flop down on a garden chaise - to be still and get just plain lazy - like an iguana in the garden.

Property Layout: This property offers a spacious 3 bedroom 2.5 bath mid-century home and a private studio cottage with renovated kitchenette and private bathroom.

Main House - The floor plan of the main house has a traditional mid-century layout with the three bedrooms and 2.5 bathrooms that are off the hall that connect to the living room.

There are two master bedrooms in the main house. The blue master bedroom has an en-suite private bath, king size bed, and little garden space for reading and relaxation. A second master bedroom across the hall offers a queen size bed and has a custom renovated en-suite bathroom that features oversize windows above the tub, glass block, with an oversized shower with seamless glass doors, oversized vanity with a black granite top, and walls finished with knotty pine and tile.

The third (spare) bedroom, also off the hall is cozy and has a view of the tropical forest green. Bedding is a trundle bed that offers one or two twins. The half bath (i.e. free-standing sink and commode) are directly across the hall from the third bedroom.

Key West City, Florida USA

Studio Cottage - The brilliantly renovated studio cottage with spacious sleeping loft, is set up as a writers retreat and is a perfect office space as well as private living area. Complete with spacious candy apple red kitchenette and private bathroom with shower, the downstairs provides a living room area with a sofa, writing desk and large flat screen TV. Climb the ladder to the loft and find a private sleeping cuddle nook with king size bed. Downstairs next to the writing desk is a twin size bed for napping or sleeping on the ground floor.

Bedding Summary:

- ➢ Main House - 1 queen size bed, 1 king size bed, and 1 trundle bed (2 twins).
- ➢ Studio Cottage - 1 king bed (in loft) 1 twin bed on first floor

Special Features: Very large swimming pool and fun outdoor cabana entertaining area; Baby Grand Piano.

Close to the beach. Renovated private studio cottage with kitchenette, bathroom, and sleeping loft.

Amenities: Large swimming pool (heat optional) with large garden, fenced yard, full kitchen, kitchen, private studio / office, A/C, W/D, color cable TV's, BBQ grill, C/D player and stereo. Linens and towels provided, easy neighborhood parking next to house. Pets allowed, restrictions apply.

Area: The property is very unique for a Key West weekly rental in that it is located in a quiet residential area away from most vacation rentals that are licensed to rent weekly. Situated on corner lot, there are neighbors only on one side. There is plenty of room to lounge at the pool in the large garden area.

Activities: Higgs Beach and Salute Restaurant on Higgs Beach, White Street Pier, Rest Beach, tennis courts, West Martello Fort (Key West Garden Club) are a 5 minute walk from the house. Down the street from the White Street Gallery nieghborhood where you find

Fausto's Fine Food Palace for groceries, shopping, galleries, and restaurant. All Old town Key West features including, museums, sailing, boating, snorkeling, diving, theatre, night life, family activities an easy bike ride away.

Restrictions: Smoke Free House. The property is located in a residential neighborhood and is definitely not suitable for staging loud parties. This property is not "child-proof". We do not accept guests less than 25 years of age unless accompanied by a family group or guardian. Pets allowed, restrictions apply.

Summertime Things to Do (on the water)

Though summertime in Key West is our tourism off-season, there is no shortage of engaging activities for the whole family. But if there's one thing any local would recommend you do in Key West, especially in the summer, it's get on the water.

Summertime in particular makes for the best boat weather. The lack of wind permits the crystal-clear waters to be glass calm, stretching miles out to our barrier reef. The water's temperature is perfect, offering a nice break from the high humidity heat. No matter your interests, experience, or skill level, there are watersport activities for everyone.

Shoobies:

The best part about these no-prior-knowledge-or-skills-required activities is that they're great for the whole family. As long as your kids can swim, they should be fine participating in any of these activities.

Parasailing
Have all the fun of parachuting without having to jump out of an airplane! Charter companies in town such as Fury and Sebago will take you out on their specially designed boats so that you can get a true bird's eye view of Key West and the surrounding waters. After harnessing you in appropriately (usually in pairs) they launch you off the back of the boat, keeping you

attached by a tow line. As the boat gains some speed and they let out some line, you'll find yourself hundreds of feet in the air gently cruising behind the boat. Often, the captain will slow the boat allowing you to gently freefall and dip your toes in the water for a bit of extra fun. Generally children under 6 are not permitted to go and those under 18 must have a parent sign their liability waiver. I loved parasailing as a kid and even got to take a bunch of friends out for my birthday one year!

Snorkel the Reef
The reef is a must see when you visit Key West. You may have noticed that the beaches in Key West are small and, frankly, not great. That is all attributed to our reef. One of the largest in the world, the Florida Keys Barrier Reef stops waves from coming in and crashing on our island. Hence, we get no surf and no waves to form natural beaches on our tiny limestone home. Our sand is imported so that we can enjoy what we know as our beaches today.

Many people who visit Key West wonder which beach is the best to snorkel at or where they can go to snorkel from shore, but the simple answer is that none of the snorkeling from shore is very great. The reef begins about 6 miles off the south side of the island, so you generally need a boat to get there. There are several charter companies that will take you out, provide gear, and show you how to snorkel and get a firsthand look at some amazing sea life. On your way out you will often see dolphins and depending on the day you can see all kinds of creatures like sea turtles, sting rays, hundreds of types of fish, and more. Check out Floridays for a great day of sailing and exploring one of the coolest ecosystems on the planet.

½ Day Fishing Charter
People know Key West all over the world for its fantastic fishing. If you're not experienced water-people, though, I would definitely recommend a half-day fishing charter as opposed to the full day. Only about five degrees north of the Tropic of Cancer, the

sun down here, especially in summer, is very strong. I see tourists every day who don't believe it, or think that they're used to the sun because they have a beach house in Long Beach, and they end up looking like a freshly boiled lobster before the end of their first day here. Apply lots of sunscreen and reapply throughout the day and you will be fine. Also if you have them, wear a long sleeve sun shirt and a hat and even a buff to cover your face. A half day charter will give you plenty of time to catch your dinner for the night but still leave you with some energy to do things once you get back to land. Plus, it's a little easier on the kids.

Paddle Board/Kayak eco-tour
Paddle boards and kayaks are some of the most relaxing ways to spend some time out on the water. Head out to Lazy Dog on Stock Island (the next island up) and take a 2-hour kayak or paddle board eco-tour. The guides will show you hands-on and teach you about the wildlife and plants right in our back yard. Plus, after the tour, you can say you've paddled from

the Atlantic Ocean to the Gulf of Mexico and back! It only amounts to about a 2-mile excursion, but your friends don't have to know that. When you get back you'll be in prime position to have a real seafood lunch at the famous Hogfish Bar and Grill on Stock Island.

Novice to intermediate:

I'd recommend these activities to adults and families who are not strangers to the water. One of the most important things for safety when in the water is the ability to be relaxed and comfortable, so having some prior time spent in the ocean, especially, is a good idea for these activities, but not an absolute requirement.

Reef Dive
For an even greater experience at the reef, stay submerged on scuba or snuba (no individual tanks) and really extend the experience. There are dive boats all over the island that do day trips including Dive Key West, Lost Reef, and several others. I got PADI certified down here to dive when I was 13 and had a great time checking out the Western Dry Rocks and Sambo Reef.

No certification is necessary to go on a chartered trip and they'll have all the gear. All you need to do is show up and keep channeling positive energy to attract some awesome critters.

Paddleboard/Kayak Rental
If you're more comfortable on the water or don't want to be in the whole group setting that comes with a tour, Lazy Dog and many other businesses around town offer kayak and paddleboard rentals where you can go off on your own. My favorite, is to rent a kayak out of Lazy Dog and head into the Riviera Canal. There you can paddle through the man-made canal and check out all the houses on the edge and on your left when you enter there are hidden little entraces into the mangroves. Once you find one, you can pull yourself through the tidal creeks (which feels like going through natural tunnels) until it opens up into the Key West Salt Ponds. There's lots of wildlife back there and you can have an awesome day of exploring and peacefulness.

Familiar Water-Seekers:

Vandenberg/Wreck diving:

For those of you who have some experience scuba diving, Key West is known to be a great diving destination. We have a number of shipwrecks in our surrounding waters that have become extraordinary artificial reefs. One of the biggest, best, and most famous is the USNS General Hoyt S. Vandenberg located about 7 miles south of Key West. After a 10-year, 75,000 man hour, $8.6 million project, the ship was finally sunk to be used as an artificial reef and dive destination. I remember playing hooky from school that day to go out and watch them perfectly sink the boat so that it sits upright on the bottom of the Atlantic Ocean. The bottom of the ship sits at 150' below the surface, with the deck at about 90', and the tops of the satellites and antennas peaking at about 50'. You're sure to see some bigger fish, including goliath grouper, black grouper, schools of jack, and even bull sharks.

Spearfishing charter

For those of you who like to dive, free dive, and fish, spearfishing is the ultimate watersport. To me, there's something so much more satisfying about getting a fish by holding your breath and swimming into its element and spearing it so that you can have some fresh dinner. Even only a mile off of Key West you can find small patch reefs with hogfish waiting for you. My favorite was to go out in the early afternoon, take a couple of short dives in only about 15' water, and come back to filet the catch for some fresh fried hogfish tacos. To be sure you find spots that meet your skill level and aren't looking for fish all day, take a half or full day charter and I can almost guarantee you'll set a personal best or two. Captain AJ Hally from Into the Blue Charters will take good care of you.

Boat rental
If you have some experience boating, particularly in the keys, there are plenty of boat rentals available. I do not recommend renting your own boat if you are not very comfortable navigating the waters. Boating in the

keys is especially difficult, because of the number of boaters, divers, and snorkelers, as well as the nature of the Gulf of Mexico. The back country, as we conchs like to call it, is very shallow and full of sandbars. You have to know where you're going and how to drive a boat properly (such as when to get up on a plane etc.) or you will be sure to run aground or destroy some wildlife. Tearing up the sea grass by running where you're not supposed to, which we see from Miami visitors frequently, leads to fines upwards of $300 per square foot damaged.

That being said, getting out on the boat on your own is a great time and will really give you the experience of feeling like a local. Check the tide chart and try to make it out to Snipes Point, where you'll find entire families, including their pets, and groups of friends of all ages enjoying the sandbar and playing games in the sun until it goes down. Run over to the west side of the island before the sun goes down to catch your own private sunset cruise before heading in.

Key West City, Florida USA

Things to Do , in Key West

The tiny island of Key West is blessed with an amazing variety of fine international cuisine, nationally recognized music and entertainment, beautiful art galleries, creative shops and services, and historic museums, parks, and gardens. In the list that follows (*in alphabetical order*) we reveal to you selections from our own personal 'well worn path' from decades of living and loving in Key West, with our hope that you may discover why, through the continual changes brought with time, we continue to love this island so much. And while we think our list is an excellent representation of some of the most fabulous and remarkable locally owned and operated establishments, in no way is it meant to exclude other equally superb local businesses.

Big Kahuna Charters
477 Drost Drive, Cudjoe Key, Florida Keys, FL 33042

- 305-304-5498 -

Back Country Flats Fishing. Home Base is in Cudjoe

Gardens, U.S. Highway 1, mile marker 21 - but Captain Chris Robinson comes to you. Captain Chris Robinson is a world-class flats fisherman guide who has been fishing the Florida Keys for over 30 years! Captain Chris takes you into the 'back country' in the Gulf of Mexico and offers absolutely the best flats fishing experience you could dream of. Regardless of your skill level, from beginner to experienced angler Captain Chris promises and delivers a premier fishing experience you will never forget!

Farout Fishing Charters
6000 Peninsular Ave 33040 Key West

(305) 747-46 -

Captain Chris Mendola has over 25 years of experience fishing and diving in the waters off the Florida Keys. Chris grew up fishing with his dad as a boy and got into commercial fishing at the age of 18. He's been a licensed captain and fishing guide for over a decade and has accumulated thousands of fishing spots producing a wide variety of fish. Key West is located between the Gulf of Mexico and Florida Straits. Because of its location there are many different species of fish he can target.

Garrison Bight Marina
711 Eisenhower Drive, Key West, FL 33040

305-294-3093 -

Contact this marina if you are bringing a boat to Key West and need a boat slip in Old Town Key West with a full service department. They also have dry dock storage, a fuel dock, bait and tackle, ice, a ships store, and boat rentals. If you want to rent a slip or rent a boat, it is best to call well in advance.

Key West Golf Club
6450 College Road, Stock Island, Key West, FL 33040

305-294-5232 -

A Rees Jones Designed public championship golf course. Very picturesque course with wild tropical views, lakes and opportunities to see Florida Keys wildlife including birds and gators. Well kept greens.

Call for Tee Times. Full service restaurant and bar. Lessons by PGA Pros.

Key West Lighthouse and Lightkeeper's Museum
938 Whitehead St., Key West, FL 33040

305-295-661 -

Visit the lighthouse museum, learn about the history, and climb the 88 steps to the top for an incredible view of Key West. The lighthouse opened in 1848 with a woman as its Keeper; nearly unheard of during the 19th century. In 1969, the U.S. Coast Guard decommissioned the Key West Lighthouse since there was no longer a need for a full-time Keeper due to technological advancements.

Key West Seaplane Charters
3475 South Roosevelt Blvd. Key West, FL 33040

305-293-9300 -

Fly to the Dry Tortugas and Historic Fort Jefferson on a seaplane. Sightseeing along the way, you see old shipwrecks, dolphins, sea turtles, and sharks from a birds eye view. Land in the pristine turquoise waters, then walk on land to explore one of the most amazing National Parks in the U.S.A. Enjoy bird watching, pristine beaches, great snorkeling, for a morning, afternoon, or full day.

Key West Sunset Celebration at Mallory Square
One Whitehead Street., Key West, FL 33040

786-565-7448 -

The Key West Sunset Celebration is a happening every evening at historic Mallory Square behind the Waterfront Playhouse. Hundreds of people gather before sunset on the boat docks everyday. With the sun setting as a back drop, street performers thrill the crowds. You'll see the likes of tight rope walkers, fire eaters, animal trainers entertaining a delighted crowd. Local arts and crafts exhibitors, and food carts are on hand for homemade snacks. You may even find a palm reader to help determine your future. Possibly a move to Key West?

Pier House Resort and Caribbean Spa
One Duval Street, Key West, FL 33040

305-296-4600
When you're looking for a relaxing day of tranquility the Caribbean Spa will help rejuvenate your body and soul. Peaceful full-service spa offering a variety of restorative therapies, including massage, facials, hair and nail, make-up, and more. Restful and beautiful tropical space.

Shakti Yoga Key West
1114 White St., Key West, FL 33040

305-587-4285

YOUR ISLAND COMMUNITY. YOUR STUDIO. FOR HOWEVER LONG YOUR STAY. Wherever you are on your path, Shakti Yoga and their instructors are committed to supporting you on your journey of health and well-being. They offer a diverse selection of classes for various levels of practitioners. Mats & props are available for your use. You may also inquire about their private & semi-private yoga instruction. The entire space is a place to go and be your most radiant self. They also offer teas, coffees, refreshing drinks and healthy fare to keep you balanced at their very own Cafe Mayanjali. Treat yourself to a renewing visit to Shakti Yoga and Mayanjali Cafe. Relax in the boutique and find earth friendly yoga gear, ayurvedic oils and a library of enlightening books on healthy lifestyles and body/mind healing. shaktikw@yahoo.comShakti

Sunset Sail Key West A private charter boat fleet in Key West, FL
202 William St, Key West, FL 33040

(305) 587-44 -

Sunset Sail Key West provides the perfect experience for couples looking for a romantic evening, friends out for some fun on the water, or a family trip. The Key West sailing adventures run during the day, sunset, and even under starlight. Unlike many other Key West sailboat charters, Sunset Sail Key West provides strictly private charters tailored to your personal desires.

Tennessee Williams Fine Arts Center
5901 College Rd. Stock Island, Key West, FL 33040

305-296-1520

Located on the campus of Florida Keys Community College. Head North like you're leaving Key West and turn at the sign for the hospital. Tennessee Williams

Theatre is Key West's state-of-the-art performing arts center for Key West that brings our island the best live, professional, nationally-touring shows and performers from New York and around the world. The theatre also features locally produced annual shows and touring road companies that bring to our island professional dance, opera, music, and New York Broadway style shows.

The Red Barn Theatre
319 Duval St., Key West, FL 33040

305-296-9911

Romantic intimate theatre. Over 25 years of live theatre in Key West, it consistently offers great live shows of all kinds. See drama, comedy, musicals, and cabaret featuring the most talented actors, dancers, theatres, and directors from Key West's own famous performing arts community. The theatre has comfortable seating, and a full bar.

Tropic Cinema
416 Eaton St., Key West, FL 33040

305-296-9493 -

Here, film is celebrated as art, and the film line up is fabulous in this local's non-profit movie theater created by the community of Key West with the goal to celebrate film and identify Key West as a haven for artistic film. The theater itself is up-beat and beautiful with a deco style lobby and wonderful lounge where you can buy wine, beer, espresso, and yummy home made treats. Most of the staff members are volunteers and everyone loves the art of film. Enjoy the two screening rooms and the main theater that seats 150.

Waterfront Playhouse
310 Wall St., Key West, FL 33040

305-294-5015 -

Located at Mallory Square, near where the Sunset Celebration is held every night. Florida's oldest continually running professional theatre group, where the "Key West Players" have been presenting the "magic of live theatre for 65 years." This theatre group prides itself on maintaining the highest professional standards and continually provides dynamic and challenging live theatre for Key West's diverse community and our tourists. The theatre has adopted Key West's official motto of 'One Human Family,' reflecting the belief of the Players that theatre has a special power to reflect and thereby illuminate the human experience by celebrating the common humanity that unites us. The Players are committed to encouraging local playwrights.

White Street Pier
Intersection of Atlantic Blvd. and White St., Key West, FL 33040

A great way to get out on the water without even getting on a boat! Undeniably the best sunrise view on the island. This is a massive concrete pedestrian pier at the foot of White Street. Sometimes called the "unfinished road to Cuba," it extends several hundred yards over the Atlantic Ocean next to Higgs Beach. Cast out a fishing line or just take the kids and dogs for a brisk morning walk. The pier juts off Higgs Beach at the bike path and the Key West Aids Memorial. Walk or ride your bike. Nice place to walk the dog.

Cultural Sights

African Slave Cemetery
1000 Atlantic Blvd., Key West, FL 33040
Key West Higgs Beach burial site memorializing 295 Africans who perished on the shores of Key West after being rescued from the slave trade when U.S. Navy boats intercepted Cuban slavers enroot to Havana in 1860 and did their best to save the would be slaves. Cement pillars that are carved with symbols of West African proverbs mark the site where at least nine Africans who died are buried here.

Archeo Gallery Key West
1208 Duval St., Key West, FL 33040
305-294-5771

Favorite authentic Key West art gallery and store on Upper Duval Street, brought to you with love for the simplicity of art created by tribal people from far reaching places. Original hand picked tribal art pieces and rugs that don't come from factories. All pieces in the store are made by real people in tribes throughout the world. In the words of the gallery owners, "When you lay your hands on any piece at Archeo you feel the echo of history. You share a moment with the creator of that piece. We invite you to bring that sense of honesty into your home."

Coffee Mill Dance Studio
916 Pohalski Lane, Key West, FL 33040
305-296-9982

Located in Old Town, Just off Truman Ave. on little lane behind the Chevron Station at the corner of Truman and White Streets. Dance, exercise, and yoga classes taught by highly professional teachers. Unique Key West Studio owned by Penny Leto who holds a university degree in Dance Education. The Coffee Mill is a long established tradition and is housed in a most charming renovated old "conch coffee mill." Drop in classes available.

East Martello Museum
3501 South Roosevelt Blvd., Key West, FL 33040

305-296-3913 -

Located across from Smathers Beach - Civil War Fort A Civil War and watch tower that began construction in 1862 by the U.S. Army to defend against a possible Confederate sea assault, but never saw battle. In credible structure, considered a monument to Civil War engineering. Explore the preserved battlement's collection of Civil War relics, learn about wrecking and cigar making in the early days. Impressive collection of sculptures by artisit Stanley Papio, and perhaps the most fun part ... meet the 'ghosts of East Martello,' and get a look at famous Robert the Doll. These are all fun for the entire family.

Ernest Hemingway Home And Museum
907 Whitehead St., Key West, FL 33040
305-294-1136

This was the home of Ernest Hemingway who lived and wrote in Key West for more than a decade. A true fishing sportsman, he loved the water off the Florida Keys and traveled and lived for many years of his life between Key West and Cuba (only 90 miles away).

Take this educational tour of his Key West home and learn more about the most prolific period of his Nobel Prize writing career. And then there are the famous 6 toes cats that freely roam the grounds. Fun and educational for the entire family.

Gallery on Greene
606 Greene St., Key West, FL 33040
305-294-1669

Long established art gallery on Greene St., featuring an extensive collecting of over 35 museum quality artists. Art for the gallery is selected that represents the local charm and island history of Key West.

Gingerbread Square Gallery
1207 Duval St., Key West, FL 33040
305-296-8900 -

Be sure to stop by and Gingerbread Square Gallery and discover the inspiring art. Located on on elegant Upper Duval St., inside a charming Victorian house with clapboard siding and window shutters. Overlooking a lovely side courtyard, Gingerbread Square Gallery recalls the genteel Key West of a simpler time of days gone by. The gallery represents a number of artists whose styles reflect Key West's tropical and multicultural flavors.

Guild Hall Gallery
614 Duval St., Key West, FL 33040
305-296-6076 -

A Key West icon in the art world. Established in 1976, Build Hall Gallery is a co-op with 27 Key West artists. Still in it's original location, it promises to stay to stay true to its original dream of providing ..."affordable spaces for Key West artists to display their work and expand their creative potential." You're sure to fall in love with something unique in this special place.

Haitian Art Company
605 Simonton St. Suite A.Key West, Fl. 33040
305-296-8932 -

Very Unique art gallery by any standards. This long established gallery store supports an incredible list of Haitian artists and is known for having the best collection of original Haitian Art in the USA.

Harrison Gallery

825 White St. Key West, FL 33040
305-294-0609

Harrison Gallery features original art by its signature artists and gallery owners, Helen and Ben Harrison who have been creating extraordinary art in Key West for over 30 years. The gallery, located on White Street, also features carefully curated pieces by other talented artists from around the world.

Historic Seaport Harbor Walk
William St. to Greene St., Key West, FL 33040
Stroll along the meandering wooden walkway on Key West's famous harbor that winds from above the foot of William Street to Greene Street. Enjoy a large variety of unique island shops, restaurants, and one-of-a-kind bars. Until 15 years ago, it was known as the 'Key West Bight' and was a working fishing harbor where the shrimp boats docked and fishermen brought in their catch. Today over 150 slips in the harbor provide dockage for private yachts and charter boats. Catch a sunset cruise, catamaran, dive boat, and gaze at Key West's own tall ship the "Western Union."

Island Arts Co-Op
1128 Duval St., Key West, FL 33040
- 305-292-9990 -

Great place to discover original arts and crafts to take home with you as a treasured memory of Key West. An established co-op of several Key West artists featuring jewelry, photography, acrylics, watercolors, oils, pottery, and all types of arts and crafts as well.

Key West Aids Memorial
1000 Atlantic Blvd., Key West, FL 33040

Located on the White Street Pier this memorial is a City of Key West Park and tribute to the people who have died of AIDS and showed their love of the Florida Keys when living, working or visiting here. More than 1,100 names are inscribed on flat granite monuments which are embedded in the walkway approaching White Street Pier at the Atlantic Ocean.

Key West Historical Grave Yard
701 Passover Ln., Key West, FL 33040
- 305-292-8177 -

Well worth taking the time to visit, this land mark

grave yard is historically informative, interesting, beautiful and fun to ride your bike or walk through. Look for the tall grave marker that says "I Told You I Was Sick", and be sure to visit the U.S.S. Maine Memorial site. Most grave sites are buried above the ground.

Tennessee Williams Fine Arts Center
5901 College Rd. Stock Island, Key West, FL 33040
- 305-296-1520 -

Located on the campus of Florida Keys Community College. Head North like you're leaving Key West and turn at the sign for the hospital. Tennessee Williams Theatre is Key West's state-of-the-art performing arts center for Key West that brings our island the best live, professional, nationally-touring shows and performers from New York and around the world. The theatre also features locally produced annual shows and touring road companies that bring to our island professional dance, opera, music, and New York Broadway style shows.

The Custom House
281 Front Street, Key West, FL 33040
- 305-295-661 -

The Custom House is the "Jewel of Key West". An incredible work of architecture, it was built in 1891 and served as a post office, court house and government center when maritime wrecking made Key West the richest city, per capita, in the U.S.A. Today it stands proudly as a museum and the home of the Key West Art and Historical Society.

The Red Barn Theatre
319 Duval St., Key West, FL 33040
- 305-296-9911 -

Romantic intimate theatre. Over 25 years of live theatre in Key West, it consistently offers great live shows of all kinds. See drama, comedy, musicals, and cabaret featuring the most talented actors, dancers, theatres, and directors from Key West's own famous performing arts community. The theatre has comfortable seating, and a full bar.

The Studios of Key West

533 Eaton St., Key West, FL 33040
- 305-296-5200

It is said that Key West has more artists and writers per capita than any other place in the United States. Some of our leading creative people and community leaders joined together to create an amazing art center called "The Studios of Key West." Art lovers should be sure to check out this unique facility. Workshops, classes, exhibitions, and performance events are scheduled regularly.

Tropic Cinema
416 Eaton St., Key West, FL 33040
- 305-296-9493 -

Here, film is celebrated as art, and the film line up is fabulous in this local's non-profit movie theater created by the community of Key West with the goal to celebrate film and identify Key West as a haven for artistic film. The theater itself is up-beat and beautiful with a deco style lobby and wonderful lounge where you can buy wine, beer, espresso, and yummy home made treats. Most of the staff members are volunteers and everyone loves the art of film. Enjoy the two screening rooms and the main theater that seats 150.

Waterfront Playhouse
310 Wall St., Key West, FL 33040
- 305-294-5015

Located at Mallory Square, near where the Sunset Celebration is held every night. Florida's oldest continually running professional theatre group, where the "Key West Players" have been presenting the "magic of live theatre for 65 years." This theatre group prides itself on maintaining the highest professional standards and continually provides dynamic and challenging live theatre for Key West's diverse community and our tourists. The theatre has adopted Key West's official motto of 'One Human Family,' reflecting the belief of the Players that theatre has a special power to reflect and thereby illuminate the human experience by celebrating the common humanity that unites us. The Players are committed to encouraging local playwrights.

Food and Drink

Key West loves a good meal as much as it loves a good party. Island cuisine offers fresh seafood, Caribbean flavors, and Key West charm.

Long acclaimed for its laid-back lifestyle and fun & funky personality, Key West is equally renowned for its wonderful restaurants and bars. The burgeoning number of established and brand new eateries have attracted award-winning chefs and rising new stars fresh from the top culinary schools who continue to make this tiny island a draw for "foodies" from all over the world.

Local dining choices range from five-star gourmet establishments to casual cafes and raw bars. From Duval Street and the waterfront, to hidden Old Town gems or the Historic Seaport, restaurants occupy old homes and other buildings featuring widely diverse architectural styles. Dining in Key West is more than just a meal it's a real experience.

Of course, frozen pina coladas and conch fritters are not what make this island a culinary paradise. The town's tropical climate and proximity to Cuba, only 90 miles away, play unmistakable roles in the creation of Key West cuisine. Fresh seafood, Florida citrus and exotic fruits figure prominently on island menus, as do plantains, black beans and other Cuban and Caribbean specialties. Be sure to stop in at one of the many little Spanish cafes to sample the inexpensive and delicious fare, or simply to try a cup of authentic café con leche (Cuban espresso with steamed milk).

Seafood is what visitors to Florida are always asking for, and Key West is certainly the star in that department. Stone crab claws, spiny lobster, and yellowtail snapper you name it: if it swims, crawls or grows in the ocean, you can be sure its on a menu in this food-loving city. Among the most sought-after Key West delicacies are pink shrimp, which are harvested from fisheries in and around the Dry Tortugas. So desirable that they are often referred to as "pink gold," these incredibly sweet shrimp are served in every style imaginable from broiled and baked to marinated, sautéed, fried and grilled. Sit down with a pound of fresh "peel 'n' eat" shrimp and a frosty mug of beer for a reasonably priced slice of Key West heaven.

Key Lime Pie
Speaking of slices, let us now pay tribute to the legendary key lime pie. So much has been said and written about this fabled signature sweet, that few people know the real deal from frozen or chain restaurant versions.

Real key lime pie is made from authentic key limes (about the size of a small egg with very tart pulp), and the true test of the product is its color: it has a yellow (not green!) custard in a pressed graham-cracker crust and tastes like nothing else.

Some restaurants top off the pie with whipped cream, but any local worth his salt knows that a lightly-browned merengue topping makes it the "real McCoy.

Casual Dining

Nearly every restaurant in Key West is casual-friendly, meaning you will be welcome wearing shorts, sandals, and t-shirts.

Key West is known for its relaxed lifestyle and not being uptight about appearances. You'll eat well while on the island no matter what your attire.

But don't hesitate to dress up a bit for a nice dinner. Many restaurants here are hip, chic, and gourmet and cleaning up a bit is often an appropriate way to dine.

Below are restaurants we classify as "Casual Dining", which encompasses nearly all of Key West's dining options.

Mellow Cafe and Gastropub
Casual craft beer bar serving tacos, sandwiches, salads and more dockside in Garrison Bight.

Sitting by the docks in Key West, enjoying a cold beer and a fresh fish taco, while watching the boats come and go. Doesn't that sound like a fine Key West experience? (It is)

Mellow Cafe and Gastropub, an off-the-beaten-path craft beer bar and eatery does a nice job of offering a casual bite in a typically Florida Keys relaxed place. When there, you might feel like you've discovered a hidden place easily missed by the masses.

The tacos, their specialty, are excellent and obviously make use of quality ingredients. And with the charter-boats nearby, there is little doubt the snapper is fresh. Salads are piled high with a garden of nutritious flavors.

Mellow Cafe also serves the best banh mi sandwich in Key West. Banh mi is a sandwich the resulted from French colonialism in Vietnam and is prepared with a crunchy roll (traditionally french baguette, but here on ciabatta), and filled with Indonesian flavors.

To pair with the tasty tacos, salads, and sandwiches is a bountiful selection of over 100 craft beers with a rotating cast of 11 on tap.

Happy hour offers generous drinks specials and a very inexpensive way to taste the menu (which is inexpensive as well).

Location: 1605 N. Roosevelt Blvd

AZUR

Modern Mediterranean cuisine, fresh high-quality ingredients, and a pleasant indoor and outdoor ambiance combine to make this inspiring restaurant a favorite of Key West Travel Guide. If you are a foodie, put this one on your list.

Located in a mostly residential section of the historic quarter of Key West, this small white-linen restaurant serves delicious food in a relaxed, yet elegant, setting.

Brunch, lunch, and dinner are all recommended. Tapas are perfect for a light snack; grilled octopus is a favorite. Raw bar "crudo" features the freshest seafood. Gnocchi are particularly good and pillow-like, and perfectly paired with braised beef and truffle drizzle. Bountiful salads and tasty sandwiches served on grilled ciabatta bread are among the delicious choices.

Location: 425 Grinnell Street

Hours: Open every day, 8am 3pm for breakfast and lunch (Saturday and Sunday brunch service begins at 9am), 6pm-10pm for dinner

Phone: (305) 292-2987

Duetto Pizza & Gelato

Delicious, authentic thin-crust Italian pizza, panini sandwiches, fresh focaccia, and more make Duetto a favorite casual restaurant in Key West

One of Key West's best pizza restaurants is Duetto Pizza & Gelato, a relative newcomer to the cuisine scene. Located downtown, just two blocks away from Sloppy Joe's and Duval Street, this is an excellent place to grab a bite.

Serving authentic Italian thin-crust pizza, freshly-baked focaccia sandwiches, pressed ciabatta sandwiches, panini, and daily housemade gelato, this small and casual pizzeria will have you returning again and again. Italian coffee drinks, fruit smoothies, and gelato milk shakes are each fantastic and worthy of a visit.

Duetto means "duet", and the magical combination of the two owners (one from Italy), results in outstanding food prepared using fresh, wholesome ingredients.

As one of our favorite pizza (and more!) options on the island, we are more than happy to add them to the Key West Travel Guide "Our Favorites" list.

Location: 540 Greene Street
Hours: Open every day, 11am 10pm
Phone: (305) 848-4981 FREE DELIVERY IN KEY WEST

OnlyWood

Believe it or not, there was a time, albeit long ago, when it was nearly impossible to find a great Key West version of three of life's most important things: pizza, bagels, and live music. Fortunately, great pizza and great music are abundant on the island (alas, you can still only get a "good" bagel). In the top tier of Key West pizza would have to be OnlyWood.

Tucked away on a hidden lane off Duval Street, this quaint and casual indoor/outdoor restaurant serves authentic Neapolitan pizza, cooked in an immense wood-fired brick oven imported from Italy, along with the highest quality Italian ingredients. House-made mozzarella cheese, a 1000-degree oven, and imported ingredients combine to make a thin-crusted, crunchy, delicious pie.

The high quality continues throughout the menu, with pasta, appetizers, and main courses that will have you convinced you are in Italy. As a result, OnlyWood is on the "Our Favorites" list of Key West Travel Guide.

Location: 613½ Rear Duval Street
Hours: Open every day, 12pm 10pm
Phone: (305) 735-4412 *FREE DELIVERY IN KEY WEST*

Thirsty Mermaid

Thirsty Mermaid is a relatively new addition to Key West's food scene, and it is a welcomed addition. One could argue that there is a new wave of Key West chefs and restaurateurs in the island re-inventing and expanding Key West cuisine. Thirsty Mermaid is definitely a member of the new renaissance.

Located one block off Duval Street, the small restaurant will make you feel like you've discovered a hidden gem.

The decor is modern, graphic, and inviting, and the menu is a nicely curated selection of fresh seafood, local flavor, and a "foodie" sensibility.

Both times we visited we were more than impressed at the quality of the dishes and ingredients. Bountiful salads, a near-perfect snapper fish sandwich, and mouth-watering appetizers had the table nodding in agreement that Thirsty Mermaid deserves a place in the "Our Favorites" section of Key West Travel Guide. Congrats!

Location: 521 Fleming Street
Hours: Open every day, 11am 11pm
Phone: (305) 204-4282

The Salty Angler

Located on the upper end of Duval Street, the Salty Angler has recently celebrated its two-year anniversary. Congratulations!

The kind and friendly chef/owners make an extra-effort so that delicious, satisfying dishes come out of the kitchen.

This newer restaurant and bar has quickly found a very dedicated local following thanks to a flavorful menu of smoked bar-b-que, fresh fish sandwiches, entrees, and a creative menu of burgers and sandwiches. Popular items include their original "Thunder Thighs", a hickory-smoked preparation of chicken thighs, the sliced brisket particularly good as a sandwich or taco, and their pulled pork. Fish items on the menu are the freshest available and all come from locally caught fish.

And if you have been out fishing in Key West, the kitchen offers to "cook your catch." Bring the cleaned fish you caught and The Salty Angler will cook it for you, grilled or blackened, for $11 per pound.

The bar itself is a friendly, laid-back atmosphere, with live music often performed, including regular shows by Key West's most talented jam band, The Happy Dog (usually Thursday nights and not to be missed).

If you are looking to have an authentic Key West experience, pop in here and see what the locals are loving.

Free delivery is available.
Location: 1114 Duval Street
Hours: Open every day, 11am-11pm (or often later, if need be)
Phone: (305) 741-7071

Sandy's Cafe

If you are looking for a low cost to-go meal, Sandy's Cafe is a convenient carry-out cafe popular with locals in Key West.

With its iconic red and white striped awnings, walk-up window service on White Street, and long line of working locals waiting for the inexpensive and satisfying sandwiches and coffee, Sandy's Cafe is, one could say, a Key West institution. Each morning Sandy's serves a steady stream of cops, city workers, tradesmen, and service industry folks a testament to its consistency, affordability, and hearty servings.

Attached to M&M laundromat (for a long time, this cafe was known as M&M's) and decidedly humble, the cooks at Sandy's quickly prepare Cuban pressed sandwiches served on fresh Cuban bread and toasted in a panini press. Favorites include the breakfast sandwiches and the Cuban Mix the unofficial sandwich of Key West and packed with sliced ham, pork, Swiss cheese, and pickles.

Cuban coffee is served. Strong espresso can be ordered in numerous sizes: the tiny and economical "bucci" is a bit bigger than a thimble's worth, a "colada" is four-times as much. Most popular is "cafe con leche," the

Cuban version of the Italian latte: espresso with steamed milk.

Sandy's stays open late-night and is a popular place for an after-Duval Street snack. You're sure to meet a local.

Location: 1026 White Street
Hours: Sunday-Thursday 5am 12am/midnight Friday, Saturday open 24 hours
Phone: 305-295-0159 (FREE DELIVERY

Date and Thyme (formerly Help Yourself)

Serving some of the healthiest food on the island, Date and Thyme is the little cafe and market that keeps surprising us with its creativity, authenticity, and motivation.

Opened just a few years ago, this little take-out cafe has gained a very loyal local following due to its dedication to fresh organic ingredients and delicious cuisine that caters to vegetarians, non-vegetarians, vegans, and gluten-free.

The cafe recently expanded and now offers an impressive market of organic groceries and green goods. Plan are to further expand to a more complete organic vegetable and fruit market.

And don't miss the Date and Thyme Smoothie bar, which blends organic frozen fruit with fresh, house-made creamy coconut milk or organic apple juice.

Food is take-out only, with tables and benches provided for you to dine and hang out.

Hours of Operation: 8am-4pm, every day
Location: 829 Fleming Street
Phone: 305-296-7766 (offers free delivery)

Mangoes

For many "foodies" visiting Key West, Mangoes is just what they are looking for…great food and a great atmosphere. The restaurant is laid out with an outdoor patio, inside dining room, tropical garden, upstairs dining rooms, and a balcony over-looking Duval Street

Mangoes Restaurant is known for "Floribbean" Cuisine, a wonderful mix of the Caribbean, local seafood and a touch of the Mediterranean.

Now under new ownership, the restaurant has been completely renovated and its menu renewed where local flavors and produce (not just mangoes!) are included. Lunch features fresh and colofrul salads, fresh fish tacos, local shrimp dishes, and hearty burgers. Dinners offer an abundance of gourmet fresh seafood and steaks.

Nice outdoor bar, as well.
Location: 700 Duval Street

Coffee Shops

Key West coffee shops serve both a social and gustatory experience and are the first places both locals and tourists find themselves on any beautiful day in Paradise.

As the name suggests, coffee houses focus on providing coffee and tea as well as an assortment of light snacks.

From a cultural standpoint, these bright and aromatic cafes largely serve as centers of of social interaction: a place to congregate, talk, write, read, entertain one another, or pass the time, alone or in informal groups that sometimes create a friendly club for its regular members.

Key West offers both small "mom and pop" cafes and well known national chains that both usually provide free WIFI service.

Start your Key West day with a delicious cup of hot java from one of these friendly establishments.

5 Brothers Grocery & Sandwich Shop

5 Brothers Grocery and Sandwich shop is located on a corner in Old Town Key West. There you will find a tiny store packed with products many of which are used in

the preparation of their homemade food. This is a friendly place where city workers, police, tradesmen, and Old Town residents mingle, grab a newspaper, and enjoy some of the most satisfying sandwiches.

Each morning the local crowd pours in for the best Cuban coffee and breakfast sandwiches. The cafe con leche (Cuban espresso with steamed milk) is strong and flavorful. Enjoy it with a Cuban cheese toast or other breakfast sandwich and you'll know why it seems that all of Old Town frequents this little shop.

If it is busy, and usually it is, a coffee line forms on the left side. If you don't want coffee, head over to the cash register and place your order. 5 Brothers serves one of the best Cuban Mixes on the island a sandwich with ham, pork, swiss, lettuce, tomato, mustard, and mayo served on Cuban bread and pressed & toasted on a hot press machine.

Location: 930 Southard Street
Hours: Open Monday to Saturday

Sloppy Joe's Bar - A Key West Tradition
201 Duval St., Key West, FL 33040
- 305-294-5300

Located at the corner of Duval and Green Street. A Key West Tradition since 1933! Sloppy Joe's is known all over the world as 'the best party in town' where folks gather for fun, food, and some of the best entertainment in Key West. At 9:00 am every morning, Sloppy's eases into the day for breakfast and beverages. By noon the live entertainment starts to warm up and when night time comes the heat turns up dancing and music and then the bar really rocks! Sloppy Joe's is also world reknowned for one-of-a-kind events like the annual Hemmingway Look Alike Contest that happens every July, and the Dropping of the Giant Conch Shell on New Years Eve. And be sure to stop into the Sloppy Joe's retail shop for souvenirs and clothing.

801 Bourbon Bar
801 Duval St., Key West, FL 33040
- 305-294-4737

Famous bar downstairs right on Duval St lovve by loyal locals and tourist fans alike. Unique Key West after-hours club upstairs with sassy talented drag show performers known for getting the crowd going. Happy Hour Specials. Come one... come all to one of Key West's most unique establishments.

A & B Lobster House (Alonzo and Berlin's)
700 Front St., Key West, FL 33040
- 305-294-5880
On the Historic Seaport Harbor Walk. Upstairs is fine dining at A&B Lobster House with House Specialties like a Surf & Turf of filet mignon and lobster tail and Black Angus Strip Steak served with a bearnaise sauce and classic favorites like Lobster Bisque. You'll also find the elegant swanky Berlin's Martini & Cigar Bar upstairs where you must at least sample a rare cigar and sip a little cognac. If you're looking for casual dining go downstairs to Alonzo's Lobster House and go for the Oysters Moscow, a seafood salad, and some chowder. Great place to view the luxury yachts docked in the harbor and watch the old Schooners come in to dock at sunset.

Abbondanza - Italian Restaurant

1208 Simonton St., Key West, FL 33040
- 305-292-1199

As the Italian name so aptly suggests...Good savory traditional Italian food served in very generous portions. Another local's favorite that is great for the family or a group of friends! Our family usually orders pasta dishes when we go there and everyone enjoys from the little kids to grandpa. And don't forget those garlic rolls. The little kids like to exclaim the name 'Abbondanza'! Prices are extremely reasonable for what you get. Atmosphere and decor is soft and has a worldly feel.

Ambrosia Sushi Key West
1401 Simonton St., Key West, FL 33040
- 305-293-0304 -

Authentic Japanese Cuisine & Sushi Bar. Outstanding fare. Absolutely stunning modern abstract upscale fashionable modern interior with waterfall and kinetic art. Both the food and décor tickle the senses. Some locals call it Key West's "gourmet sushi bar."

Antonia's
615 Duval St., Key West, FL 33040

- 305-294-6565 -

Known for outstanding food and service. Big open spacious dining room creates a lively yet intimate atmosphere. Great spot to plan a dinner for a large group. Full bar. Established Key West favorite and always a sure bet for full fare Fine Italian dining. Great wine selection. (We alternate between La Trattoria and Antonia's for Italian and love them both - but you have to be sure to go to the gym or run along the beach if you do this on a regular basis!)

B.O.'s Fish Wagon
801 Caroline St., Key West, FL 33040
- 305-294-927 -

Since 1988 Buddy Owen (B.O.) has been servin' up one of the very best island fresh fish sandwiches in Key West. Don't be shocked when you first see this cookin' shack - this is real Key West authentic and worth the stop. B.O. starts with the freshest local fish (usually grouper or mahi mahi) he can find and melds it with special Key Lime Sauce on fresh baked Cuban Bread and the melt-in-your-mouth taste scrumptious! Dishes are served up with some fresh cabbage slaw and fries. For another delicious Caribbean style treat go for the conch fritters. Wine, beer, variety of non-alcoholic drinks.

Banana Cafe
1215 Duval St., Key West, FL 33040
- 305-294-7227 -
Authentic Cuisine Francaise. A definite must! Open for breakfast and lunch = my favorite place to indulge in brunch. Owner chef Dani is from France and knows the art of creating the perfect food with the perfect setting for breakfast and lunch par excellence. The menu is fresh, pure, and the scene is so relaxing it is easy for locals to take it for granted. Crepes and sauces are the best you will find any where, delicious sandwiches on French baguette, delightful salads, fresh squeezed juices, champagne and coffee. Set in newly renovated building overlooking Upper Duval St, you can sit inside or outside on the porch looking to beautiful gallery stores with a slow parade of people strolling by. Go for

brunch and have a mimosa. And chase it with a cafe au lait. Friendly staff and excellent service.

Blue Heaven ~ World Famous
729 Thomas St., Key WEst, FL 33040
- 305-296-8666 -
You really haven't had a true Key West dining experience until you try this. Without a doubt one of Key West's most unique and most popular restaurants. Come to Bahama Village and dine under the trees in an artist's village among the resident cats and... yes.. Key West chickens - there is inside seating too. Gourmet food is excellent, flavorful, colorful and always fresh. I love the fresh fish dishes the best. Wine Spectator has given this unique restaurant its Award of Excellence! Full Bar in the tree Garden, plus a gallery and gift store featuring local artists. One of most memorable dining experiences you will ever have.

Cafe Marquesa
600 Fleming St., Key West, FL 33040
- 305-292-1919 -
1st-Class talented chefs offer beautiful presentations of select "Classic Contemporary American" gourmet

cuisine at Key West's finest Marquesa Hotel in classy intimate dining setting in 5-Star Hotel down town Old Town. They make a mean martini too.

Cafe Sole
1029 Southard St., Key West, FL 33040
- 305-294-0230 -
Romantic intimate little French-Caribbean restaurant in residential neighborhood famous for locally caught seafood embellished with a French mastery of sauces. Chef John Correa refined his skills in France and created a unique Key West menu unlike any on the island. Famous for his preparation of rare hog snapper, and yellow tail, he also offers authentic classic preparations like Duck L'Orange, Rack of Lamb, and Lobster Bouillaise. Great wine selection. Indoor and outdoor garden seating. Excellent service.

Camille's Restaurant
1202 Simonton St., Key West, FL 33040
- 305-296-4811 -
Just one block off Upper Duval St.: I eat at Camille's consistently more than any other restaurant in town. This restaurant has been voted a locals favorite for

years and years - breakfast, lunch, and dinner. Owner Denise Chelekis describes their fare as "Exotic Family Cooking with No Boundaries." Menu changes daily - chef is inspired and makes some of the best hollandaise sauce you will ever taste, and his soups are noteworthy. Go for the eggs-benedict, and choose from traditional to smoked salmon. Take the family or meet up with friends. Delightful decor. Excellent cafe con leche. Full bar, great wine selection. Private room available for special events.

Chico's Cantina - Mexican Restaurant
5230 U.S. 1, Stock Island, Key West, FL 33040
- 305-296-4714 -
Located at mile marker 4.5 just over the Cow Key Channel Bridge from Key West, on Stock Island. Family owned and operated this is a Key West tradition since 1984 and a memorable place to enjoy a wide array of authentic Mexican food. A favorite with local families (this is always a first choice when our whole family, from grand kids to grand parents, go out together for lunch or dinner). Menu features their locally famous

fine fajitas and they pride themselves on offering Mexican specialties not to be found in other restaurants. I love the seafood tacos and portabella mushroom enchiladas. Their guacamole and salsa is unbelievably fresh and delicious ...and then there is the sangria! Atmosphere is fun. Service is outstanding! Friendly staff members greet guests as welcome friends. It's worth the 15 min. drive from Old Town.

Croissants De France
816 Duval St., Key West, Fl 33040
- 305 294 2624 -
A touch of Paris in Key West, and Yes, the owners are French! Delightful housemade pastries.Things that make me go mmmmm...Paris brest, a choux pastry with a hazelnut cream or a Fraisier with vanilla mousseline and strawberries. Going to the beach? Grab a sandwich and tart combo and don't forget a piece of quiche with spinach and mushrooms. Bistro is open for breakfast and lunch. Exquisite cakes for weddings and birthdays.

Date & Thyme

829 Fleming St.
- 305-296-7766 -
Outstanding taste and nutrition. Outstanding 'build your own meal' walk-up health food restaurant. Homemade organic breads, smoothies, fresh coffee. Food is always extremely fresh and delicious. The food is so healthy that I feel the food bliss right after I eat! On Saturday there is a 'sidewalk market' where you can by fresh produce.

El Meson De Pepe's - Authentic Cuban Food in Mallory Square
410 Wall St., Key West, FL 33040
- 305-295-2620 -
Fabulous food, a full bar (try a mohito), and a live Salsa band right on Mallory Square in the heart of the action! For over 20 years Chef Pepe Diaz and his Cuban family "have been dedicated to great quality food and the preservation of Cuban-Conch Heritage in Key West." This is the place for a real Cuban cultural experience where you can enjoy real Cuban Conch cooking with real Cuban Conch hospitality ... with the added feature of amazing live and lively Latin Music

and dancing. Inside and outside seating. Celebrate the Cuban way! A most unique Key West restaurant experience.

El Siboney Restaurant
900 Catherine St., Key West, FL 33040
- 305-296-4184 -
'Siboney' is a town in Cuba, and this delightful section of Key West was at one time a little "Cuban Town". There are still may Cuban families living in this authentic Key West neighborhood and you simply MUST GO HERE for authentic Cuban fare. Locals consider it the best Cuban restaurant on the island, and everything is good and protions are generous. Be sure to try their plantains and yuka. I love their fish preparations. Inside seating in renovated brick house in south side residential neighborhood. Be sure to take your appetite with you. Wonderful friendly family service! Best to make reservations.

Faustos Fine Food Palace - On Fleming St.
522 Fleming St., Key West, FL 33040
- 305-296-5663 -

Located on the North side of the island. Locally owned and operated for generations the Weekly family. These wonderful markets have almost everything, including great produce, fine wines, butcher shop, sushi, and made-to-order deli. This location delivers groceries and will fax you a shopping list!

Faustos Fine Food Palace - On White St.
1102 White St., Key West, FL 33040
- 305-294-5221 -
Located on the South side of the island. Locally owned and operated for generations the Weekly family. These wonderful markets have almost everything, including great produce, fine wines, butcher shop, sushi, and made-to-order deli.

Five Brothers Grocery and Take-Out Cuban Coffee
930 Southard St., Key West, FL 33040
- 305-296-5205 -
Serving Key West for over 30 years! All styles of authentic Cuban made-to-order Cuban coffee at it's very best! Wonderful walk-up/take-out counter with awesome Cuban breakfast and lunch treats inside a great little tiny family owned Cuban Grocery Store, so

you can shop while your cafe is made. Neighbors stumble in for their wake up brew. Try bouchi, cortadito, cafe con leche, Cuban sandwiches.

Flamingo Crossing Ice Cream Store
1105 Duval St., Key West, FL 33040
- 305-296-6124
Outrageously delicious homemade creamy ice cream and clear sorbets made on premises. There are so many flavors to choose from you just must look for yourself. My favorites are mango sorbet, Cuban coffee, and Mangrove Honey-Walnut, and of course... chocolate. Set in an old Key West "conch house" the ambience is authentic as the treats. This is a Key West ritual for locals and should definitely become part of your Key West routine while you are here. This is right next door to the Key West Grand Vin wine bar, and I guess I must admit a favorite decadent indulgence is to go for wine... and then a little later have some ice cream. Yowsa!

Glazed Donuts
420 Eaton St, Key West, FL 33040

- 305 924 9142 -
Voted one of USA Today's ten best places. This is the fine dining of donuts! Baked daily from scratch with fresh seasonal ingredients. Light fluffy donuts, lip lickin' good. Try the Key Lime or Maple Bacon. Wash down with a coffee or a more indulgent mimosa.

Goldman's Deli
2796 North Roosevelt Blvd, Key West, FL 33040
- 305-294-3354 -
A fantastic authentic Bagel Deli owned and operated by the Goldman family. Open for breakfast and lunch, everything made from scratch and absolutely fresh bagels are made on premises daily "...boiled and baked, the old fashioned way." Deli sandwiches, grill featuring the reuben and grilled kosher frank, and smoked fish platters, slaws, potato salad, and fabulous special items including yummy potato latkes served with sour cream and applesauce, and potato knish! My favorite breakfast is the lox spread and scallion omelet, and for lunch I love the nova-scotia smoked salmon platter...or the tuna nicoise. In New Town at the

Overseas Market. You'll see this shopping center as you head out of town. (It is across the street from Home Depot).

Grand Vin
1107 Duval St.
- 305-296-1020 -
Located at Upper Duval St. near the corner of Virginia St. Best kept secret spot. Local's favorite! Incredible Wine Selection, go there to stock up! Right next door to "Flamingo Crossing" where you get the best ice cream so you can walk next door for a scoop of your favorite ice cream... and then go back for more wine. The owners (McConnell family) are world travelers and very knowledgeable purveyors offering an impressive selection of wines. Charming and island authentic intimate wine bar located in renovated Victorian house is great fun for wine tasting or drinking a bottle or two. Purveyors are frequently there and wonderful to meet and visit with. Romantic "Casa Blanca" atmosphere.

Harpoon Harry's ~ Restaurant and Bar
832 Caroline Street, Key West, FL 33040

Key West City, Florida USA

- 305-294-8744 -

Many Key West local characters meet here 'bright and early' for breakfast everyday and the late risers make it for lunch. This is a real slice of Key West life where you'll see 'The Piano Man,' Capt. Dave, Dink Bruce, and a regular selection of colorful characters and artists - mixed in with other locals, military, and tourists lucky enough to find the place. Whether you're looking for a big pile of French Toast with powdered sugar, biscuits and sausage gravy, a fresh fruit cup, a scrumptious sandwich, or just a cup of strong cafe con leche and maybe a stiff Bloody Mary, you'll get it here. Real authentic Key West restaurant right on the Key West Historic Seaport at the Key West Harbor Walk. Great atmosphere, outstanding service, full bar. Open at night too so you can sit and watch the harbor as you cocktail.

Hog's Breath Saloon
400 Front St., Key West, FL 33040
- 305-296-4222 -

World famous saloon and eatery, popular with locals and tourists. Outstanding live music entertainment, great drinks, and delicious raw bar with local seafood and grill. Live music daily from 12:00pm - 2:00 am. Fun clothing outlet for Hogs Breath T-Shits and Hats - remember "Hogs Breath is Better than No Breath at All."

Hurricane Hole Bar and Seafood Grill
5130 Overseas Highway
- 305-294-0200 -
On the docks ocean side. Be sure to go here for original Florida Keys ambience and real fresh fish, shrimp, and lobster, all locally caught! Eat dock side or upstairs in the restaurant. Hang out on the docks and chat with the local fishermen and watch the "catch' as it comes off the boats and heads to the kitchen. No frozen or imported products are ever served at Hurricane Joe's. Popular with locals and tourists of all ages and attitudes. We like to go there with the whole family from grandkids up.On US on the ocean side, on Stock Island. Quick drive from Old Town.

Kennedy Cafe

924 Kennedy Drive, Key West, FL 33040
- 305 809 9000 -

If you are venturing into New Town for shopping, or exploring the Island away from Old Town, this restaurant is a great pit stop. Definitely a locals' eatery. Don't be put off by the basic decor. Uzbekistan/Mediterranean fare. Some of my favourites...Lamb Gyro, meatballs and Greek salad, baklava and house made Turkish bread. Anything I have had here has always been fresh and delicious. They also deliver.

Key West Golf Club

6450 College Road, Stock Island, Key West, FL 33040
- 305-294-5232 -

A Rees Jones Designed public championship golf course. Very picturesque course with wild tropical views, lakes and opportunities to see Florida Keys wildlife including birds and gators. Well kept greens. Call for Tee Times. Full service restaurant and bar. Lessons by PGA Pros.

Key West Sunset Celebration at Mallory Square

One Whitehead Street., Key West, FL 33040
- 786-565-7448 -

The Key West Sunset Celebration is a happening every evening at historic Mallory Square behind the Waterfront Playhouse. Hundreds of people gather before sunset on the boat docks everyday. With the sun setting as a back drop, street performers thrill the crowds. You'll see the likes of tight rope walkers, fire eaters, animal trainers entertaining a delighted crowd. Local arts and crafts exhibitors, and food carts are on hand for homemade snacks. You may even find a palm reader to help determine your future. Possibly a move to Key West?

La te da
1125 Duval St., Key West, FL 33040
- 305-296-6706 -

A Key West and long time favorite for over 30 years, La te da is recognized internationally by discriminating travelers as a preferred destination. Beautifully housed in a landmark building La te da is a sort of 'multi-dimensional' resort offering a first-class restaurant with elegant dining, 3 different bars that include the

"By George" piano bar in inside in the front, the "Terrace Bar" on the porch overlooking Duval St., and the "Crystal Bar" upstairs in the in the dramatic state-of-the-art show space... the "Crystal Room Cabaret". If you've never been to the "Crystal Room Cabaret" you must go to experience some of the best Cabaret you will see anywhere. Our best-of-the-best Key West performers include the famous entertainers Randy Roberts, Bobby Nesbitt, and Bruce Moore.

La Trattoria - A Taste of Italy
524 Duval St. and 3593 S. Roosevelt Blvd., Key West, FL 33040
- 305-296-1075 -
Two locations - Duval Street and overlooking the Atlantic Ocean. Fine Italian dining. Wonderful food, excellent atmosphere ~ feels a little like being in Italy. A perfect place for a special night out to celebrate a birthday or anniversary. Everything is delicious and I always have a hard time choosing. Great wine selection. Street side dining room and bar with great view of Duval St. stays open late with a limited menu. It

adjoins Virgilio's bar in the back on Applerouth Lane, a local's favorite music venue and outstanding chocolate martinis.

Latitudes on Sunset Key
245 Front Street Westin Key West Resort Key West, FL 33040
- 305 292 5394 -
Upscale fine dining, perfect for that special occasion. Take a ferry across to romantic Sunset Key. Dine beachfront, whilst listening to the waves lap the shore. White tablecloths and tiki torches add to the ambiance. You truly feel like you are in Paradise. Superb menu, great seafood dishes. Love the fish tacos for lunch and scallops for dinner. Reservations are a must to get you on the ferry across.

Louie's Backyard Restaurant
700 Waddell St., Key West, FL 33040
- 305-294-1061 -
The finest ocean front dining experience, this special place is a favorite with locals, visitors, and must-stop for celebrity guests such as Jimmy Buffet. Executive Chef Doug Shook offers award winning fine

international / Caribbean Cuisine with a specialty in locally caught fish. I love his Poached Eggs with Blue Crab Cakes and Roasted Chile Hollandaise, and Florida Lobster Braised in Truffle Butter with Spinach.

Mangia Mangia Pasta Cafe
900 Southard St., Key West, FL 33040
- 305-294-2469 -
Fresh homemade pasta made on premises everyday and the sauces are 'to die for' with so much to choose - from marinara, to meat sauce, from alfredo to seafood sauces. Their Broccoli Rabe is famous and don't miss their Burschetta marinated in extra virgin olive oil. Set in a unique and one of the most charming old renovated Victorian homes in residential neighborhood. Eat in the house or out in the patio garden. Great wine bar and fine wine selection. Very popular with locals and tourists - there always seems to be a line of people spilling out the door. Excellent friendly service.

Mangoes
700 Duval St., Key West, FL 33040

- 305-292-4606 -

A Key West tradition this ever popular downtown restaurant continues to give locals and tourist alike tropical dining at its best. In the open-air, and on the highly visible corner of Duval and Angela Streets this is the best place in town to eat and see-and-be-seen. Big outdoor patio space covered with large dining umbrellas. Air conditioned inside seating plus the added feature of a "secret" upstairs local scene. Great outside bar overlooking the street.

Martin's
917 Duval St., Key West, FL 33040
- 305-295-0111 -

Martin's has been on Key West for over 20 years, has a definite local following, and has always remained one of my all time favorite places to eat a decadent gourmet Sunday brunch and drink espresso and mimosas at the same time. The gourmet eggs benedict menu is fantastically unique. I usually go for the crab cake eggs benedict and my husband usually goes for the filet mignon or black forest eggs benedict. They're also well known for their Bellini's and they have some very delicious German dishes and they have a fabulous French Toast. Martin's new location on Duval St. has a very chic island-cosmopolitan flare with both inside and outside with a view of Duval St. plus intimate garden dining in the back. Open for breakfast, lunch, and dinner. Upscale happy hour! Reservations can be made on opentable.com

Michaels Restaurant
532 Margaret Street, Key West, FL 33040
- 305-295-1300 -
If a mouth watering steak is on your mind go here. Michaels' steaks are 100% prime beef, flown in from Chicago by particular chef owners of this outstanding establishment, Michael and Melanie Wilson. Excellent fresh seafood specialties, with selections that change nightly, depending on the best catch of the day. This is a first-class steak house in a charming remodeled cottage and garden setting in residential neighborhood off Southard St. One of the finer Key West restaurants.

Local's favorite. Full bar in the garden. You can also get fondue at the bar. Excellent service.

Nine One Five
915 Duval, Key West, FL 33040
- 305-296-0669 -
Don't Miss This One!! Created by owner Stuart Kemp, this fine European style tapas restaurant is a recent winner of the James Beard Foundation Award for culinary excellence in New York. Located in a gorgeously renovated Victorian house with minimalist elegant interior, this is a great place to 'see-and-be-seen' on the town. The creative chef offers an eclectic variety of tapas, and full fare of gourmet food and fine wine selection to choose from. Everything is delicious. One of my all time favorites is the Tuna Dome. Dining inside or outside on the porches the overlook Upper Duval St. Great retro-design club room upstairs overlooking Duval St., 'Point 5', can be rented for private events. Excellent service. Friendly attentive staff.

Origami Japanese Restaurant

1075 Duval St C3, Key West, FL 33040
- 305-294-0092 -
Feels like home to me. Located in Duval Square. Casual dining, you can belly up to the bar. Eat inside or in the fabulous plaza garden complete with tall shade tree garden and talking parrots in the back ground. Sushi Bar, tempura, teriyaki. Local's favorite. Kiyoto, Owner & chef - 20 years in Key West.

Pepe's Cafe
806 Caroline Street, Key West, FL 33040
- 305-294-7192 -
Right on the famous Key West Historic Seaport near the Key West Harbor Walk. Absolutely some of the best casual island charm of any of our Key West establishments - for some folks this special spot IS Key West dining! Sitting in the courtyard under a giant tree with a crystal chandelier makes me feel a little like I am in St. Barth's and sitting inside reminds me of a wooden pub in Bermuda. One of Key West's oldest and consistently popular establishments. 'Caribbean American' gourmet style fare - from omelets to home-style soups, from juicy burgers and steaks to fresh fish.

The best fresh squeezed orange juice, and did I say GREAT Bloody Mary's to start the day! Full Bar.

Pier House Resort and Caribbean Spa
One Duval Street, Key West, FL 33040
- 305-296-4600 -
When you're looking for a relaxing day of tranquility the Caribbean Spa will help rejuvenate your body and soul. Peaceful full-service spa offering a variety of restorative therapies, including massage, facials, hair and nail, make-up, and more. Restful and beautiful tropical space.

Salute on the Beach
1000 Atlantic Blvd, Key West, FL 33040
- 305-292-1117 -
Right on Higgs Beach near West Martello Gardens - A must experience ... Key West Unique! Fun and Caribbean laid back festive casual beach atmosphere is created in a special beach-scene setting like none other on the island - or nowhere else in the U.S. for that matter! Enjoy a fabulous view of the ocean on the South-side of the island of Key West. Fun to watch beach volley ball players in the daytime. Great fusion

of fresh food choices, for brunch, lunch, and dinner. Full bar. Good choice to meet up with friends and family.

Sandy's Cafe - The Original Cuban Sandwich - Bucci Too!!
1026 White St., Key West, FL 33040
- 305-295-0159 -
Wonderful walk-up/ take-out made to order outstanding Cuban cafe. Sleepy locals meet to wake up early in the morning. Get a bouchi (Cuban espresso - they call it "Cuban Speed.") I'm addicted to the Cortadito, a pre-sugared cafecito topped with just a teeny bit of steamed milk. It's really strong so if you are not used to the "punch" you may want to try a cafe con leche first. Get the buttered Cuban toast or cheese toast and dunk it in the coffee for a great start on the day. For lunch try the locally famous mouth watering Cuban Mix sandwich or a scrambled egg with melted cheese and fresh tomato. They also have unbelievably delicious chicken tacos! Connected to M&M Laundry so you can wash and sip. Now open 24 hours.

Santiago's Bodega
207 Petronia, Key West, FL 33040
- 305-296-7691 -
So much fun! New-Age / Tropical-European Dining Experience. Gourmet tapas menu, excellent food. The delicious sangria flows and you can choose red or white. Fashionable intimate dining room with romantic club-like atmosphere and you can also sit outside on the covered porch and watch real life in Bahama Village go by. Excellent service with friendly staff. Reservations recommended.

Schooner Wharf Bar - "The Last Little Piece of Old Key West"
202 William St., Key West, FL 33040
- 305-292-3302 -
Located at the foot of William St. Right on the Key West Historic Harbor Walk. Authentic famous seafarer's Key West open-air waterfront Bar that some call "The Last Little Piece of Old Key West". Originally created on the private old schooner "Diamante" owned by Evalena and Paul Worthington in the '70's, the bar was moved ashore dockside when the Historic Seaport

was still a working waterfront. Open-air, fun, funky, live music daily, specialty drinks, and a great bar menu from omelets to chowder, to fantastic Raw Bar and more. "Sailors headquarters" and favorite local bar.

Seven Fish
632 Olivia St., Key West, FL 33040
- 305-296-7777 -
A hometown bistro - Key West fish-style, in an 'off-beat' residential neighborhood (just off Truman Ave.) Intimate setting that is sort of a Euro-Caribbean scene. Go for the fresh local fish and sashimi and if your heart is set on meat (or meatloaf) you can get that too. And be sure to try their extraordinary Banana Chicken. Local's favorite Key West restaurant. Intimate setting in Heart of authentic Old Town Key West historic residential neighborhood. Best to make a reservation. New Grand Truman Street location coming in 2016.

Sippin Coffee House and Internet Cafe
424 Eaton St., Key West, FL 33040
- 305-293-0555 -
Coffee and Internet Cafe. Great freshly brewed Americana coffee made to order and sweet treats.

Several computers with internet access. Nice comfortable large roomy space for catching up on email, computer work, reading, and quiet chat. Close to the main downtown Post Office.

Small Chef At Large
725 Poorhouse Lane • Key West, FL 33040
- 305-294-1493 -
Catering, Private Chef Services and Provisions. One of Key West's very favorite catering companies features well regarded chefs Jennifer and Alice who have been cooking on this island for a long time. If you are looking to cater a wedding reception, private party, fundraising event, or order in you favorite holiday meal for Thanksgiving or Christmas dinner, check out their palate stimulating menus. Only the freshest gourmet foods are used in their preparations.

Square Grouper Bar & Grill
MM 22.5 ("Up The Keys") 226558 Overseas Hwy, Summerland Key
- 305-745-8880
Located on Summerland Key at MM 22.5 on the ocean side. It seems to pop up out of nowhere, so keep your

eyes peeled or you can easily drive by it. This place gets consistent rave reviews. Whenever we drive home from a trip to Miami, we always stop at the Square Grouper for dinner for a fresh seafood dinner. The food is varied and fantastic - something for every taste and artistically presented. The atmosphere is beautiful and service is great. We've enjoyed intimate dinners and also taken the family for special occasions.

Sugar Apple Cafe and Market
917 Simonton St., Key West, FL 33040
- 305-229-0043 -
Locally owned and operated - Key West's oldest, most established, and best selection of homeopathic remedies, vitamins, organic produce, gourmet vegetarian cafe deli, and juice bar. Nutritional advisor on staff. Yes, it is possible to live healthy in paradise.

Tavern N' Town located in Key West Marriott Beachside Hotel
3841 N Roosevelt Blvd, Key West, FL 33040
- (305) 296-81 -
A local favorite for top notch cuisine. The best lobster mac & cheese in Key West! The ambiance, high

ceilings, and spacious seating area make you feel like you are at a royal dinner party. Be sure to stop by for Happy Hour and enjoy a handcrafted cocktail from the bar while listening to the musical delight of local artists

The Afterdeck Bar
700 Waddell St., Key West, FL 33040
- 305-294-1061 -
The After Deck has a long and famous history, and 'ritual grounds' where seasoned colorful 'old time' Key West characters convene to ponder the events of the day. Jimmy Buffet's early songs were inspired and written. This is special spot on this earth with a rare view and intimate feel of the ocean. Sunset, moonrise, and star gazing experiences are unsurpassed. I go for sunset cocktail hour several times a week. It's the perfect place to take a breath and ponder the good things in life.

The Cafe - A Mostly Vegetarian Place
509 Southard St., Key West, FL 33040
- 305-296-5515 -
Best to make reservations. Take out also available - Delicious fresh vegetarian food and homemade breads

including many Vegan choices served fresh daily. But believe me, you don't have to be vegetarian to love this food. Great grilled sandwich selections include Portobello, Mozzarella, Eggplant and Zucchini. I love their salads and their portions are so generous that I take half home for later. The family recipe for fruity sangria is loved by the regulars and if you're thinking fresh fish, she also serves a great seared yellow fin tuna with wasabi sauce.

The Green Parrot Bar
601 Whitehead St., Key West, FL 33040
- 305-294-6133 -
Established in 1890 this Landmark saloon is the oldest drinking establishment in Key West and maintains all the sinful charm and of its original open-air flare where they boldly boast "No Cover, No Minimum, No Wonder". Most hail The Green Parrot as the best music venue we have on the island. On stage you find not only the best bands in town but national touring acts. On the corner of Southard and Whitehead Streets. Fantastic place to dance your heart out. It rocks!!

Tropic Cinema
416 Eaton St., Key West, FL 33040
- 305-296-9493 -
Here, film is celebrated as art, and the film line up is fabulous in this local's non-profit movie theater created by the community of Key West with the goal to celebrate film and identify Key West as a haven for artistic film. The theater itself is up-beat and beautiful with a deco style lobby and wonderful lounge where you can buy wine, beer, espresso, and yummy home made treats. Most of the staff members are volunteers and everyone loves the art of film. Enjoy the two screening rooms and the main theater that seats 150.

Turtle Kraals - Authentic Key West Restaurant on the Waterfront
One Lands End Village, Key West, FL 33040
- 305-294-2640 -
Right on the Key West Historic Seaport Harbor Walk. An established Key West tradition it was originally a turtle canning factory (when that was legal), then just 15 years ago there was still a rehab hospital for injured turtles (when that was still allowed) and you could

have lunch while you checked out the recovering turtles. Those days are long gone but the food is still really good "southern-Style" breakfast, lunch, and dinner featuring real pit BBQ, and now there is a Turtle Museum. My how times have changed! There's a great bar upstairs with a wonderful panoramic view of authentic old Key West Historic Seaport and another full bar downstairs inside ... and they have espresso and cappuccino too.

Virgilio's
524 Duval St., Key West, FL 33040
- 305-296-8118 -
Located just off Duval Street, 1/2 block from Southard St. on Appelrouth Lane. Fabulous island charm with 2 intimate bars - one indoors and one outdoors where you can go see-and-be seen. Favorite local rock and Caribbean bands play fantastic dance music inside and outside you can sip and watch the scene. Some nights there are local D-Jays. Famous for the espresso and chocolate martinis.

Shopping

Sloppy Joe's Bar - A Key West Tradition
201 Duval St., Key West, FL 33040
- 305-294-5300 -
Located at the corner of Duval and Green Street. A Key West Tradition since 1933! Sloppy Joe's is known all over the world as 'the best party in town' where folks gather for fun, food, and some of the best entertainment in Key West. At 9:00 am every morning, Sloppy's eases into the day for breakfast and beverages. By noon the live entertainment starts to warm up and when night time comes the heat turns up dancing and music and then the bar really rocks! Sloppy Joe's is also world reknowned for one-of-a-kind events like the annual Hemmingway Look Alike Contest that happens every July, and the Dropping of the Giant Conch Shell on New Years Eve. And be sure to stop into the Sloppy Joe's retail shop for souvenirs and clothing.

Amri - Unique Salon, Spa, Boutique
1204 Simonton St., Key West, FL 33040
- 305-292-4000 -

Amri is a day spa, salon, boutique located in Key West. Amri your tropical destination if you are looking for a relaxing day or if you are looking for sustainable apparel and beauty products

Archeo Gallery Key West
1208 Duval St., Key West, FL 33040
- 305-294-5771 -
Favorite authentic Key West art gallery and store on Upper Duval Street, brought to you with love for the simplicity of art created by tribal people from far reaching places. Original hand picked tribal art pieces and rugs that don't come from factories. All pieces in the store are made by real people in tribes throughout the world. In the words of the gallery owners, "When you lay your hands on any piece at Archeo you feel the echo of history. You share a moment with the creator of that piece. We invite you to bring that sense of honesty into your home."

Assortment
514 Fleming St.
- 305-294-4066

Assortment is an established Key West tradition offering, a fine assortment of men's clothing for fashion conscious dressers, and unique gift items in an upscale sophisticated boutique setting. Claude Reams is a long-time retailer of men's fine clothing in Key West offering select casual ware, active ware, and swim ware for the discerning client. No time to pack for your Key West trip...no problem. You'll find it at Assortment!

Besame Mucho
315 Petronia St.
- 305-294-1928 -
A most unique and delightfully elegant apothecary, treasure, and souvenir store. You would expect to find a place like this in a picturesque village in the South of Spain. Located in Key West's Bahama Village, Besame Mucho offers an amazing collection of fine European toiletries and hand picked gifts that instantly feel like heirloom treasures. My daughter usually buys me something here for my birthday every year and I continue to treasure everything I've received. Once you

fall in love with this store I promise you'll want to visit the on-line shopping option. Stop in for a real treat to your senses.

Blue
718 Caroline St.
- 305-292-5172 -
A beautiful selection of fun-and-flirty island lifestyle clothing and accessories for the fashion conscious. Specializing in casual elegance you'll find exactly what you need from fashion tees to cocktail dresses to beautiful intimate apparel. Beautiful choices for women of all ages, you'll find the outfit you need at Blue. So don't worry if your home base wardrobe is void of tropical clothes - you'll find it here in Key West - no problem.

Blue Heaven ~ World Famous
729 Thomas St., Key WEst, FL 33040
- 305-296-8666 -
You really haven't had a true Key West dining experience until you try this. Without a doubt one of Key West's most unique and most popular restaurants. Come to Bahama Village and dine under the trees in an

artist's village among the resident cats and... yes.. Key West chickens - there is inside seating too. Gourmet food is excellent, flavorful, colorful and always fresh. I love the fresh fish dishes the best. Wine Spectator has given this unique restaurant its Award of Excellence! Full Bar in the tree Garden, plus a gallery and gift store featuring local artists. One of most memorable dining experiences you will ever have.

Date & Thyme
829 Fleming St.
- 305-296-7766 -
Outstanding taste and nutrition. Outstanding 'build your own meal' walk-up health food restaurant. Homemade organic breads, smoothies, fresh coffee. Food is always extremely fresh and delicious. The food is so healthy that I feel the food bliss right after I eat! On Saturday there is a 'sidewalk market' where you can by fresh produce.

Dog 30
1025 White Street, Key West, FL 33040
- 305-296-4848 -

Dog 30 is a premier pet supply store in Key West Florida. Offering only the finest brands of dog and cat food available. Plus a large selection of high quality leashes, collars, beds, toys and treats (and so much more!)

East Martello Museum
3501 South Roosevelt Blvd., Key West, FL 33040
- 305-296-3913 -
Located across from Smathers Beach - Civil War Fort A Civil War and watch tower that began construction in 1862 by the U.S. Army to defend against a possible Confederate sea assault, but never saw battle. In credible structure, considered a monument to Civil War engineering. Explore the preserved battlement's collection of Civil War relics, learn about wrecking and cigar making in the early days. Impressive collection of sculptures by artisit Stanley Papio, and perhaps the most fun part ... meet the 'ghosts of East Martello,' and get a look at famous Robert the Doll. These are all fun for the entire family.

Ernest Hemingway Home And Museum

907 Whitehead St., Key West, FL 33040
- 305-294-1136 -
This was the home of Ernest Hemingway who lived and wrote in Key West for more than a decade. A true fishing sportsman, he loved the water off the Florida Keys and traveled and lived for many years of his life between Key West and Cuba (only 90 miles away). Take this educational tour of his Key West home and learn more about the most prolific period of his Nobel Prize writing career. And then there are the famous 6 toes cats that freely roam the grounds. Fun and educational for the entire family.

Fast Buck at Home
726 Caroline St., Key West, FL 33040
- 305-294-1304 -
Exquisite home furnishings featuring unique one-of-a-kind finds made by owner Tony Falcone. Interior designer is on premises to assist you creating your dream-come-true Key West tropical home.

Faustos Fine Food Palace - On Fleming St.
522 Fleming St., Key West, FL 33040
- 305-296-5663 -

Located on the North side of the island. Locally owned and operated for generations the Weekly family. These wonderful markets have almost everything, including great produce, fine wines, butcher shop, sushi, and made-to-order deli. This location delivers groceries and will fax you a shopping list!

Faustos Fine Food Palace - On White St.
1102 White St., Key West, FL 33040
- 305-294-5221 -
Located on the South side of the island. Locally owned and operated for generations the Weekly family. These wonderful markets have almost everything, including great produce, fine wines, butcher shop, sushi, and made-to-order deli.

Fishbusterz Retail Seafood Market
6406 Maloney Ave, Stock Island, Key West, FL 33040
- 305-294-6456 -
If you want the freshest wild fish you can find, the you need to go right to the fish house and buy it. Fish is caught daily and brought to the docks by professional commercial fisherman of the Florida Keys. This authentic fish house specializes in spiny lobster,

shrimp, stone crab, grouper, snapper, swordfish, and more and more. This is an authentic 'old fashioned' Florida Keys fish house. Worth the 15 minute drive from Old Town Key West.You can also purchase fish from their on-line market, "straight from the ocean and delivered directly to your door.

Five Brothers Grocery and Take-Out Cuban Coffee
930 Southard St., Key West, FL 33040
- 305-296-5205 -
Serving Key West for over 30 years! All styles of authentic Cuban made-to-order Cuban coffee at it's very best! Wonderful walk-up/take-out counter with awesome Cuban breakfast and lunch treats inside a great little tiny family owned Cuban Grocery Store, so you can shop while your cafe is made. Neighbors stumble in for their wake up brew. Try bouchi, cortadito, cafe con leche, Cuban sandwiches.<

Gallery on Greene
606 Greene St., Key West, FL 33040
- 305-294-1669 -
Long established art gallery on Greene St., featuring an extensive collecting of over 35 museum quality artists.

Art for the gallery is selected that represents the local charm and island history of Key West.

Gingerbread Square Gallery
1207 Duval St., Key West, FL 33040
- 305-296-8900 -
Be sure to stop by and Gingerbread Square Gallery and discover the inspiring art. Located on on elegant Upper Duval St., inside a charming Victorian house with clapboard siding and window shutters. Overlooking a lovely side courtyard, Gingerbread Square Gallery recalls the genteel Key West of a simpler time of days gone by. The gallery represents a number of artists whose styles reflect Key West's tropical and multicultural flavors.

Glass Reunions
825 Duval St.
- 305-294-1720 -
A contemporary American Glass Company' has almost every kind of outrageous glass gift you can think of. Jewelry, kaleidoscopes, lamps, accessories, paperweights, perfume bottles, stemware and more. A local's Key West favorite.

Guild Hall Gallery
614 Duval St., Key West, FL 33040
- 305-296-6076 -
A Key West icon in the art world. Established in 1976, Build Hall Gallery is a co-op with 27 Key West artists. Still in it's original location, it promises to stay to stay true to its original dream of providing ..."affordable spaces for Key West artists to display their work and expand their creative potential." You're sure to fall in love with something unique in this special place.

Haitian Art Company
605 Simonton St. Suite A.Key West, Fl. 33040
- 305-296-8932 -
Very Unique art gallery by any standards. This long established gallery store supports an incredible list of Haitian artists and is known for having the best collection of original Haitian Art in the USA.

Hands On - Exquisite Clothing and Accessories
1206 Duval St., Key West, FL 33040
- 305-296-7399 -
Four extraordinary women, with a shared vision have combined their vision to create an special store offering unique artful clothing and accessories. "What

brought them together was mutual admiration of art-to-wear and accessories, as well as a commitment to making unique fashion accessible in the Florida Keys."

Harrison Gallery
825 White St. Key West, FL 33040
- 305-294-0609 -
Harrison Gallery features original art by its signature artists and gallery owners, Helen and Ben Harrison who have been creating extraordinary art in Key West for over 30 years. The gallery, located on White Street, also features carefully curated pieces by other talented artists from around the world.

Historic Seaport Harbor Walk
William St. to Greene St., Key West, FL 33040
Stroll along the meandering wooden walkway on Key West's famous harbor that winds from above the foot of William Street to Greene Street. Enjoy a large variety of unique island shops, restaurants, and one-of-a-kind bars. Until 15 years ago, it was known as the 'Key West Bight' and was a working fishing harbor where the shrimp boats docked and fishermen brought in their

catch. Today over 150 slips in the harbor provide dockage for private yachts and charter boats. Catch a sunset cruise, catamaran, dive boat, and gaze at Key West's own tall ship the "Western Union."

Island Arts Co-Op
1128 Duval St., Key West, FL 33040
- 305-292-9990 -
Great place to discover original arts and crafts to take home with you as a treasured memory of Key West. An established co-op of several Key West artists featuring jewelry, photography, acrylics, watercolors, oils, pottery, and all types of arts and crafts as well.

Key Accents
804 Caroline St.
- 305-293-8555 -
Located on the Key West Historic Seaport. If you are crazy about home design like me you probably can't resist buying a Key West gift for your home. A beautiful shop housed in an old turn-of-the-century conch house offering a wide array of fine furnishings and decorative accessories. If you own a home in Key West be sure to ask about the customized home design and decorator

services offered by owner / operator Patty O'Conner. Her expertise and professionalism in interior design make the whole experience absolutely carefree for you with simply marvelous results. Trust your slice of island paradise to a local pro!

Key West Golf Club
6450 College Road, Stock Island, Key West, FL 33040
- 305-294-5232 -
A Rees Jones Designed public championship golf course. Very picturesque course with wild tropical views, lakes and opportunities to see Florida Keys wildlife including birds and gators. Well kept greens. Call for Tee Times. Full service restaurant and bar. Lessons by PGA Pros.

Key West Lighthouse And Lightkeeper's Museum
938 Whitehead St., Key West, FL 33040
- 305-295-661 -
Visit the lighthouse museum, learn about the history, and climb the 88 steps to the top for an incredible view of Key West. The lighthouse opened in 1848 with a woman as its Keeper; nearly unheard of during the 19th century. In 1969, the U.S. Coast Guard

decommissioned the Key West Lighthouse since there was no longer a need for a full-time Keeper due to technological advancements.

Key West Sunset Celebration at Mallory Square
One Whitehead Street., Key West, FL 33040
- 786-565-7448 -
The Key West Sunset Celebration is a happening every evening at historic Mallory Square behind the Waterfront Playhouse. Hundreds of people gather before sunset on the boat docks everyday. With the sun setting as a back drop, street performers thrill the crowds. You'll see the likes of tight rope walkers, fire eaters, animal trainers entertaining a delighted crowd. Local arts and crafts exhibitors, and food carts are on hand for homemade snacks. You may even find a palm reader to help determine your future. Possibly a move to Key West?

Key West Tropical Forest and Botanical Garden
5210 College Road, Stock Island, Key West, FL 33040
- 305-296-1504 -
The only "frost-free" botanical garden in the continental United States. Our most treasured "large"

green space with great board walk trails in a unique tropical forest that holds two of the last remaining fresh water ponds in the Keys. This garden is a major migratory stopping point for tropical birds from places as far as South America. Bring the entire family.

Local Color
276 Margaret St.
- 305-292-3635 -
Established in 1986 by world cruising sailors who chose Key West to be their permanent home, they decided to meet the local demand for beautiful yet comfortable imported clothing such as Jams World, imported light weight sophisticated linen, sunglasses, hats, and artistic island jewelry including the famous KW Bracelet. This popular boutique is a long time favorite of locals and tourists alike. Seasoned success over the years expanded the store to several locations throughout the island. Check them all out at Local Color (Jewelry Stand): 425 Greene Street, and Commotion: 800 Caroline Street., and Lili's On Greene Street:424 Greene Street.

Neptune Designs
301 Duval St., Key West, FL 33040
- 305-294-8131 -
Jay and Carmenza Pfahl have been creating both traditional and imaginative fine jewelry for Key West locals and tourists alike since 1977. Their creations include a variety of meticulously crafted styles and lines of 14 Karat gold and silver jewelry, and mounted reproduction Spanish treasure coins. Jay sets all types of diamonds, gemstones, and pearls, and specializes in custom made jewelry projects and loves to collaborate with his clients to create special fantasy pieces. In addition to jewelry making, Jay is a well respected long time serious Key West orchid collector and grower. His in-depth knowledge of and appreciation for the orchid has been the inspiration for some amazing artistically fashioned orchid jewelry. If you are thinking about a jewelry purchase, be sure to put Neptune Designs on your to-do list.

Old Town Wine and Spirits
1029 Truman Ave.
- 305-294-4123

A local's favorite - Good selection of liquor and wines. Adjacent to Teasers Strip Club - (Don't let this scare you - there are separate entrances!).

Pier House Resort and Caribbean Spa
One Duval Street, Key West, FL 33040
- 305-296-4600 -
When you're looking for a relaxing day of tranquility the Caribbean Spa will help rejuvenate your body and soul. Peaceful full-service spa offering a variety of restorative therapies, including massage, facials, hair and nail, make-up, and more. Restful and beautiful tropical space.

Royal Furniture
3326 N. Roosevelt Blvd., Key West, FL 33040
- 305-295-6400 -
This is fantastic furniture and decorating resource that is utilized by both individuals and commercial businesses throughout the Florida Keys. Professional interior designers lead by Christopher Elwell, are extremely knowledgeable and offer fast and friendly service to get your home looking beautiful at reasonable prices. Great service for out-of-town part

time residents that need to furnish a vacation property and get the job done fast!

Sugar Apple Cafe and Market
917 Simonton St., Key West, FL 33040
- 305-229-0043 -
Locally owned and operated - Key West's oldest, most established, and best selection of homeopathic remedies, vitamins, organic produce, gourmet vegetarian cafe deli, and juice bar. Nutritional advisor on staff. Yes, it is possible to live healthy in paradise.

The Custom House
281 Front Street, Key West, FL 33040
- 305-295-661 -
The Custom House is the "Jewel of Key West". An incredible work of architecture, it was built in 1891 and served as a post office, court house and government center when maritime wrecking made Key West the richest city, per capita, in the U.S.A. Today it stands proudly as a museum and the home of the Key West Art and Historical Society.

The Green Parrot Bar
601 Whitehead St., Key West, FL 33040

- 305-294-6133 -

Established in 1890 this Landmark saloon is the oldest drinking establishment in Key West and maintains all the sinful charm and of its original open-air flare where they boldly boast "No Cover, No Minimum, No Wonder". Most hail The Green Parrot as the best music venue we have on the island. On stage you find not only the best bands in town but national touring acts. On the corner of Southard and Whitehead Streets. Fantastic place to dance your heart out. It rocks!!

The Key West Butterfly and Nature Conservatory
1316 Duval St., Key West, FL 33040
- 305-296-2988 -

Rare Experiential Event! This is one of the most unique and memorable attractions I have ever experienced. Housed in a large climate controlled glass arboretum with beautiful tropical foliage and flowers and inspiring background music, you feel like you are in a fairy-tale or living a magical dream. Stroll though the winding path that meanders around the giant indoor garden taking you over a trickling stream and through a gazebo where you can rest and take it all in. A unique opportunity to experience a close up view of living butterflies while they sip on flower nectar, gently fly around, and even land on you. The entire butterfly experience is accompanied by colorful little chirping finches and tropical turtles slowly walking by. There is also an educational room to learn about butterflies and a gift shop. A must see in Key West.

Key West Wedding Information

The happiest day of both your lives should take place in one of the most gorgeous places in the world, Key West! There are truly are no weddings like those that take place here in Key West. The beautiful pristine beaches and turquoise waters make a perfect setting for you to exchange your vows. There are numerous places of worship throughout Key West to accommodate people of all faiths. From large formal cathedrals to small, intimate and personal chapels, there are many wedding venues for you to choose from.

There are also many private wedding boats, schooners, and catamarans that provide wedding ceremony services for a beautiful wedding event on the water. Along with great ceremony venues, there are also endless options for reception locations. The wide array of ballrooms, guesthouses, restaurants and resorts, and also historic properties which are perfect for garden weddings and are famous for their beautiful tropical flowers and trees.

Additionally, there are wonderful Key West beaches for beach weddings and museums that will make selecting a reception venue not only a delight, but a breeze as well. Consult your Key West wedding planner for details and availability. Destination weddings are now more than ever very popular and Key West has all the professional wedding services and supplies that you will need to make your special day absolutely perfect. There are numerous florists, bakeries, Key West wedding photographers, and wedding coordinators available to assist you in your wedding needs. And don't forget the Key West wedding officiant who will be happy to help with most everything, even your Key West wedding license!

Activities

Dolphin Encounters

Schools of wild dolphins inhabit the waters surrounding Key West. Several small companies are available to take you out in search of these magical creatures in their natural habitat. Dolphin are so common in the Key West area that one specific location is often referred to as the "dolphin playground".

Dolphins are curious, friendly, yet wild mammals that are protected by stringent federal regulations. Visitors are not allowed to feed, touch or swim with dolphins in Key West. They may, however, come up to the boat and frolic and jump for your pleasure and leave you overjoyed at this unforgettable meeting.

After your visit to the dolphin playground, your guide will then take you to some wonderful backcountry snorkeling spots to see live coral, sponges, and colorful tropical fish. Snorkeling equipment and instruction are included.

Keep in mind that dolphins are wild animals, and although the captains do an excellent job of finding them each day, their presence is never guaranteed. Still, the pristine beauty of their home will never disappoint.

Call us toll-free at 877-INFO KEY (877-463-6539)

Dry Tortugas

Approximately 70 miles west of Key West lies beautiful Dry Tortugas National Park and Ft. Jefferson. This remote part of the Florida Keys is accessible only by private vessel, high-speed ferry, or seaplane.

Visitors are drawn to this spot by its fascinating history as well as its gorgeous beaches. The trip to the stark, yet stunning islands crosses incredibly clear waters where shipwrecks and sea life are usually visible. Divers, snorkelers and nature lovers flock to the area for its coral formations, loggerhead turtles, French angel fish and many rare birds.

The Spanish explorer Ponce de Leon first discovered this island chain in 1513 and called them Las Tortugas, meaning The Turtles, for the great number of sea turtles found there. The latter name, Dry Tortugas, was intended to warn seafarers that the islands contain no fresh water.

On Garden Key, the largest island in the group, you'll find historic Ft. Jefferson once envisioned as the largest link in America's coastal defense system. Its original purpose was to control navigation into the vast Gulf of Mexico and protect the Atlantic-bound Mississippi River trade from piracy. Begun In 1846, it used 16 million bricks making it the largest masonry structure in the Western Hemisphere although it was never actually finished. You can travel to its remnants today in America's most remote and least visited national park.

With remarkable snorkeling, thousands of migratory birds, and endless ocean vistas, you will never forget the sense of wonder that comes from visiting a sight seen by only a lucky few.

Fishing

Fishing is outstanding any time of the year in the Florida Keys. The rich watery expanse surrounding the islands draw millions of devoted anglers every year who thrill to the chase and anticipate the victory of catching the fish of a lifetime.

Whether your desires lean to big-game fishing, sport fishing, flats fishing, kayak fishing or party boat fishing there is a terrific experience waiting for you and your entire family. We book all of the different fishing packages in Key West and have our list of Captains and

Charterboats that know how to make our guests happy.

We'll hook you up with a top-notch charter captain to guide you on a fishing trip of your dreams. They will advise you of the best seasons for many of the most popular species found in our local waters.

We know and book the very best charter boats and the most knowledgeable guides in Key West. Many hold national and world records for their specialty

Glassbottom Boats

Key West glass bottom boat trips show you the reef through glass windows.

On this family-friendly trip, you will enjoy a leisurely ride out to sea, surrounded by the beautiful tropical water of Key West. Then, the vessel will float above the coral reef giving you a close-up look at this diverse and fascinating ecosystem.

Comfortably relax and enjoy the view as huge schools of tropical fish flash by, followed by turtles, stingrays and the occasional bottle-nose dolphin who call this stunning landscape their home.

Take a camera along for the adventure you never know what you'll see.

Golf

The Key West Golf Club, home to the only public golf course in the lower and middle Keys, is a unique, challenging, and certainly fun round of golf. Above all, the setting is stunning. The course is filled with palms, mangroves, and other tropical plants. Egrets, herons, pelicans, and many other birds are often enjoying the water hazards. And, believe it or not, tarpon are often seen "rolling" on the surface of the ponds.

This 18 hole, par-70 course measures over 5800 yards from the middle tees (6500 from the back tees). Each nine holes has one par-5, and two par-3s. Overall, the course plays more challenging than it reads on paper.

The course has a lot of wide open drives and big fairways. So golfers are easily lured into using the big stick, a.k.a. the driver. But lot's of water hazards, sand, tight and sometimes long approaches, deep rough, and unforgiving mangrove forests (a black hole: never does the ball kick out), add more than a few extra strokes. Often times, keeping the Big Bertha in the bag will be a good idea. Then again, when else are you going to drive the green on a par 4?

Directions to the golf course from Key West:

Take US1 Highway out of Key West. Turn left at the first light (on the other side of the Cow Key Channel Bride). Continue 1 mile and enter Key West Golf Club course at 6450 E. College Road (on the right-hand side.)

Greens and other fees:

Golf Rates	High Season: 10/25-5/31	Low Season: 5/1-10/31
18 Holes	$95.00	$70.00

Key West City, Florida USA

Early Bird (back-9, 7:00 - 8:30 a.m.)	70.00	70.00
Twilight	70.00	50.00
Super-twilight	n/a	n/a
Rider Fee 18 holes	30.00	30.00
Junior under 18	50.00	40.00

Above rates include green & cart fees. SOFT SPIKES REQUIRED Golf club rentals: $40.00 (PREMIUM FULL SET)

General tips:

- Summertime is very hot, and a noon-time tee-off can be brutal. With long days that time of year, play early or late. And, drink plenty of water.
- The mangroves rarely kick a ball back out. And don't think of going in after it. Mosquitoes and muck await the uninformed.
- The putting greens can play really slow or quickly. And the sandy substrate can make for a

bumpy roll. Practice putting to get a feel for the greens.

➢ Replace your divots with a scoop of sand from your cart. Keep play moving along. Though breaking up may be hard to do, that ball didn't really love you anyway.

➢ Have fun! Playing a round of golf in paradise should be a treat and enjoyed. Our best wishes!

Kayak Tours

There may be no place as ideal for kayaking as Key West. With a diverse eco-system, winding mangrove passageways, and calm shallow water, the Florida Keys provide easy and rewarding kayaking. Beginners will enjoy the easy introduction to the sport. Experts will marvel at all they can explore.

The barrier reef of the Keys results in calm and clear water near the islands. Paddlers enjoy a relaxing pace as they explore and take-in the beauty of the natural environment. Red, Black, and White Mangrove create unique landscapes and are home to many interesting organisms. Fish, stingrays, lobster, conch, and many other creatures will fascinate anyone who takes the time to look. The number and diversity of birds will astound as well.

Guided tours are transported to the backcountry aboard a traditional skipjack schooner for a morning or afternoon eco-tour in a group of up to 18 people.

Sunset Sails

Many visitors agree that the most beautiful way to observe our famous sunset is from the water, enjoying some Key West sailing down to the Southernmost Point, and toasting the end of another magical day.

It is a popular activity. While you are sailing you will be see a fleet of Key West sailboats on the water each admiring the view of the variety of boats, the on-board music, and the deeply hued setting sun.

You may choose from a sleek modern catamaran, an historic tall sail schooner, a glass-bottom boat, or your very own privately chartered boat. Whichever fits your mood or budget, they generally will all provide unlimited beer, wine, sodas and, of course, champagne for the duration of the two hour trips.

Sunset at Mallory Square

Few places in the world offer the sheer brilliance, the majesty, and the peacefulness of the Keys when it's that special time for the sun to disappear below the horizon.

Sunset in Old Town is a time honored happening when hundreds of people gather on the docks of historic Mallory Square. That's where you'll see flame tossing jugglers, a Key West sword swallower, tightrope walkers, an exotic trained bird show and "Golden Elvis" and his sidekick, "Silver Man" all the while being serenaded by assorted minstrels and the "Southernmost Bagpiper". Immediately next door, over a small footbridge, the acts continue where some of the most intriguing and locally famous acts, such as Dominique and His Flying House Cats, Speed Bump the Pig and Bounce and OOOLaLa.

If you're hungry, food vendors set up booths offering conch fritters, key limeade and other strictly homemade goodies. You'll laugh out loud as the legendary "Cookie Lady" promotes her warm delicacies while squawking slogans in perfect rhyme. There is no admission charge to the nightly celebration, but try to arrive thirty minutes prior to sunset to appreciate the full experience.

Below are the Key West sunset times, arranged for the 15th and 30th of each month:

Key West Sunset Times

Month	15th	30th
January	6:00	6:11
February	6:22	6:30

March	7:36	7:43
April	7:49	7:56
May	8:04	8:11
June	8:17	8:20
July	8:18	8:12
August	8:01	7:47
September	7:31	7:15
October	7:00	6:48
November	5:40	5:38
December	5:41	5:49

African Cemetery at Higgs Beach

Among modern Key West's greatest characteristics is its inclusiveness. But you may not realize that Key West has historically been an oasis of diversity. During the Civil War, Key West remained in the United States despite Florida having joined the secession. African

Americans on the island lived as free men long before it became the law of the land.

Make no mistake of it, though Key West did have its faults when it came to early race relations, especially when judged from our modern day expectations.

One of the earliest events highlighting the compassion of the island is memorialized at Higgs Beach, adjacent to the West Martello Fort and near the White Street Pier.

Here, you will find a sobering memorial of the astonishing story of the nearly 300 people who died after being rescued from slave ships plying their illegal trade near the island on their way to Cuba.

Depicted on the surface of the installation is a map of the Atlantic Ocean showing the slave trade routes and locations where the slave ships were captured.

Audubon House & Garden

The Audubon House Museum was established in 1960 by Key West native, Colonel Michell Wolfson, and his wife Frances. They saved and restored the historic building which had been the family home of Captain John Geiger, Key West's first Harbor pilot. He had made his fortune as a wrecking master salvaging ships that foundered on the treacherous reefs.

This elegant 1846 example of American Classic Revival architecture is a perfect setting for the work of one of America's first truly original artists, John James Audubon, who visited the home while working on his famous bird images. The style of the house and Audubon's art represent the new flowering of American design that flourished in the early 19th century.

A wonderful tropical garden in the back is very enjoyable with collections of orchids, palm trees, and lilly pool.

Self guided audio tours daily. Their gallery of antique lithographs is across the street, and for collectors and admirers or Audubon's work, it is well worth a visit.

Museum

Firehouse Museum

Key West's Old Town neighborhood is the largest collection of historic wooden structures in the United States. These treasured buildings, each dry as kindling, have survived for almost two-hundred years thanks to the brave and hard work of Key West's fire departments. The newly opened Key West Firehouse Museum, in the historic Firehouse No. 3 circa 1907 and one of the oldest firehouses in Florida, does an outstanding job of documenting the history and artifacts of the island's fire departments. The cigar industry is also prominently discussed since, in the 1890's, Key West made more cigars than the rest of the world combined, and fires had numerous impacts on the industry.

In 1875, Key West created its first City fire department using a largely volunteer force. During the 19th century, Key West fought fires using salt water as it is more effective than fresh water in fighting fires. A system of wells and steam-driven pump trucks, developed in 1888, did a good job of keeping fires from spreading.

But there were two devastating fires in early Key West, and each led to advancements and investment in the island's firefighting capabilities.

"The 1859 Fire"

The first big fire was in 1859 when much of the commercial district at that time was burned to the ground. Started in a warehouse under suspicious circumstances, the fire was stopped only by the incredible action of one person, Henry Mulrennon. He saw the fire was likely to continue its march across town. With a keg of gun powder, he blew up his own house on the corner of Fitzpatrick and Greene Street (shown on the map to the right), thereby creating a fire break.

After this fire, the city mandated metal shingle roofs for newly built structures in this part of town.

But with the rest of the town still clad in wooden shingle roofs, an even larger fire was about to destroy nearly all of Key West.

"The Great Fire of 1886"

The Great Fire of 1886 was Key West's largest and most devestating fire. The blaze began in a cafe next to the San Carlos building on Duval Street, at the time a three story wooden structure where Cuban revolutionaries plotted the overthrow of Spain. Some believe it was Spanish loyalists who set fire to the San Carlos. Regardless who started it, within 12 hours fourty-percent of the city had burned, including eighty-percent of the commercial area. Seven people died and fifteen were injured. Seventeen
cigar factories were destroyed. City Hall and most of its

records were incinerated. The only thing that stopped the inferno was the Gulf of Mexico. The entire working shoreline burned to the ground.

Before 1940, there was no running household water in Key West. Instead, cisterns collected rain water for drinking, cooking, and bathing. The Key West Fire Station No. 3 had a roof-mounted cistern, and was the only place on the island where one could take a shower.

"Gato Fire"

In 1915, one of Key West's largest cigar factories burned. Thanks to advancements in fire fighting capabilities, this fire was largely contained to the structure. The building was replaced with the stone and concrete structure on the corner of Simonton and Amelia Street. Today it is home to Monroe County's offices, and its lobby has an excellent interpretive display of Key West's cigar industry.

"Where is Bum Farto?"

Key West being Key West, the history is also filled with colorful characters. None more so than Joseph "Bum" Farto, the chief of police from 1964-1975. Chief Farto's father was the owner of Sloppy Joe's building. The young Farto was known for hanging around the nearby fire house, and became adept at bumming change hence the "Bum" nickname, considered by locals as one of endearment. In 1975, Bum was found guilty on serious narcotics charges, but refused to co-operate with authorities about

accomplices. Just before sentencing in 1976, Bum disappeared, setting off speculation. Had he been murdered by a criminal organization? Had he fled the country? Ten days after his disappearance, Bum Farto's rental car was found in Miami. He has not been seen since. For years a headline, or t-shirt, often stated "Where is Bum Farto?" to the amusement of visitors and locals alike.

Flagler Station & Overseas Railway Historium

In 1905 Henry Flagler, one of the wealthiest men in the world, announced his plan to build a railway from Miami to Key West. Some laughed, some scoffed, and most agreed that it could not be done.

Eight years, three hurricanes, thirty million dollars, and hundreds of lives lost, Flagler proved them wrong.

Visit the museum and experience the thrill of riding down the Florida Keys in 1929 aboard the "railway that went to the sea". Learn about the Key West Extension, and the tragic demise of Flagler's dream in the devestating Labor Day hurricane of 1935.

Plan to spend at least 30 minutes to see all the exhibits.
Location: Corner of Caroline Street and Margaret Street.
Hours: Open every day, 9:30 am 3:30 pm
Cost: $3 per adult, $2 per child (FREE if you have a ticket stub from the Conch Tour Train or the Old Town Trolley)

Custom's House

Key West City, Florida USA

Built in 1891, this magnificent red brick building, known locally as the Custom House, is a 3 ½ story Romanesque style landmark which first served as the city's Federal Building during the wrecking era. The waterfront building's bright red roof is iconic and easily spotted from a distance, especially by boaters.

We highly recommend a visit here.

The recently completed $9 million restoration transformed it into a first class museum with fine art & history exhibits. Currently exhibitions include Ernest Hemingway, folk artist Mario Sanchez, and railroad-builder Henry Flagler.

Hours: Open daily 9:30 am 4:30 pm. (except Christmas)
Cost: $7 per adult, $6 per senior, $5 per child, and FREE for children under 6.
Phone: 305-295-6616
Location: 281 Front Street

Shipwreck Museum

At one point in it's history, Key West was the richest city in the United States of America. Wrecking, or the salvaging of ships run aground on the reef, was big business in the 19th century.

Meet the men who risked their lives and fortunes as you enter the unique world of an 1856 wrecker's warehouse. You'll meet the master wrecker and his crew in a warehouse filled with booty and bounty of the reefs and cargo from the past.

Then climb the lookout towers, originally used by salvors to observe wrecks on the reef, and enjoy a view of the historic district and the waters that surround Key West.

This is a museum that the whole family can enjoy.
Location: 1 Whitehead Street
Hours: Open every day, 9:40 am to 5:00 pm.
Cost: Adults $15.04, Senior $12.90, Children $8.59, Children 3 & under FREE

Florida Keys Eco-Discovery Center

Key West City, Florida USA

A terrific educational facility with over 6,400 square feet of exhibits, including a 74-seat movie theater.

Highlights of the Center include an interactive map of the Keys, a replica of the Aquarius underwater laboratory, and an underwater video camera that allows guests to observe coral spawning, assess damage from a boat grounding or monitor the health of a coral reef.

The Center also features a high-definition film by renowned cinematographer Bob Talbot, computer interactive exhibits, murals, graphic displays with text and images, a live weather station and replicas of South Florida habitats such as mangroves, complete with sounds.

Mote Marine Laboratory's Baby Conch Farm has moved to the Eco-Discovery Center and is now part of its Living Reef exhibit.

The Center, located in Truman Annex, is open 9:00 a.m. to 4:00 p.m., Tuesday through Saturday and is free to the public.

And they have free on-site parking!
This is a fun thing to do in Key West for the whole family.
Hours: Open Tuesday through Saturday, 9 am 4 pm (closed Sunday and Monday)
Cost: FREE
Phone: 305-809-4751
Location: 35 E. Quay Road at the Truman Waterfront located at the end of Southard Street.

Mel Fisher Maritime Museum

World famous treasure salvor Mel Fisher uncovered the 1622 wreck of the Spanish galleon Atocha in 1985, after an exhausting search which took over 18 years and cost him the life of his son, a professional diver.

The world of shipwreck archaeology is the theme of this awesome museum where you will see the ropes of pure gold and fist-sized emeralds that were recovered. Lift a real gold bar and view a number of artifacts.

They continue to look for more treasure, and repeat Mel's famous saying "Today's the day".
You may never look into the ocean the same way again.

Location: 200 Greene St.
Hours: Open Monday-Friday 8:30am-5:00pm and Saturday-Sunday 9:30am 5:00pm.
Cost: Adults $12.50, Students $10.50, Children $6.25

Oldest House Museum & Garden

This conch cottage is known as the oldest house on the island and was built in 1829. It was home to the wrecker Captain Francis B. Watlington, his wife Emeline, and their nine daughters.

The property has three buildings, the main house, the kitchen house, and the exhibit pavillion which face a garden with benches.

On display, along with the maritime artifacts are works of art by Mario Sanchez, Key West's famous folk art wood carver.
Location: 322 Duval Street
Hours: Open daily 10am-4pm, closed Sunday & Wednesday
Cost: FREE
Phone: 305-294-9501

Turtle Kraals Museum

In the mid to late 1800s Key West was the center for turtle processing and canning. At that time, turtle soup was considered a delicacy in parts of the United States and especially in Europe.

Turtles caught throughout the Caribbean were shipped to Key West, kept alive by cruelly placing them on their backs aboard the turtle schooner ADAMS. Upon arrival in Key West, turtles were kept in dockside corrals called 'kraals' until they were slaughtered and processed into soup.

By 1970 the turtle population had been devastated. Through the courageous efforts of visionary conservationists, in cooperation with the Governor of Florida, the first catch size regulations were enacted on March 23rd, 1971, establishing that any turtle smaller than 41 inches was to be released. Turtle canneries went out of business, and the turtle trade came to an end in '71 with the passage of the Endangered Species Act.

Caribbean turtle populations have somewhat recovered but continue to struggle against natural and man made, life threatening obstacles. Destruction of habitat, reckless disposal of consumable waste products, poorly maintained traps and nets, improperly discarded monofilament and the degradation of marine waters through chemical spillage and improper discharge continue to threaten these vulnerable and gentle creatures of the sea.

Many locals genuinly care about the well being of sea turtles and the museum does a good job of informing the public about past and present dangers.

Location: 200 Margaret Street

Hemingway House

Located at the corner of Whitehead and Olivia St. is the former residence of revered American novelist Ernest Hemingway.

Hidden behind a fortress-like old brick wall is this grand home where he wrote many of his most famous works.

Well versed docents lead regularly scheduled tours through the house filled with priceless mementos and out to the expansive lawn with the writing shack and inhabited by the 6-toed cats reputed to be the direct descendants of the legendary author's kitties.

Hours: Open from 9-5 daily. Open 365 days of the year.
Location: 907 Whitehead Street
Cost: $13 per adult. $6 per child. FREE for children 5 & under.
Phone: 305-294-1575

Truman's Little White House

Harry Truman found this tropical island the perfect winter getaway.

He chose this West Indian style dwelling to be his working winter "White House" for his vacations from 1946-1952.

Truman loved being outdoors in Key West. In the morning he would often go to the beach. Also, he was an avid fisherman and whenever he could he loved to fish the Key West waters.

Situated on the former Navy property known as Truman Annex, with entrance through the Presidential Gates on Whitehead St., it has been restored with total authenticity.

Guided tours daily. Also offers a free self-guided botanical tour.
Open 9-5.
111 Front Street

Key West Lighthouse & Keeper's Museum

Built in 1847 to 46 feet high, the Key West lighthouse was later extended to 85 feet in 1894 . This Key West icon originally ran on oil, but in 1927 was converted into an "electric torch" beacon.

By 1969, the lighthouse was decommissioned and after changing hands with the local historical society, opened to the public in 1989.

Today you can climb the 88 steps to the observation deck for one of the best views of the island and the beautiful water surrounding it. We highly recommend it.

The museum is an excellent historical site with many artifacts of the era and stories of the keepers that lived there. The quarters, grounds, and the lighthouse itself have all been faithfully restored.

Hours: Open daily 9:30 am 4:30 pm (except Christmas)
Cost: $10 per adult, $9 per senior, $5 per child, FREE for children under 6.
Phone: 305-295-6616
Location: 938 Whitehead Street

East Martello

Key West, being one of the most important strategic locations for the early United States, had a series of large brick forts built along the southern shore.

East Martello was one of them, and today houses an impressive museum of early island artifacts, eclectic folk art, and treasures from the sea. One of the museums strangest and most photographed exhibits is Robert the Doll, a Victorian era cloth doll that is purported to be haunted. Many visitors claim that photographs of the doll end up with streaks of light through the picture.

Located next to the Key West airport at the eastern end of the island, East Martello is well worth visiting for anyone interested in the rich history of Key West.

Audubon House & Garden

The Audubon House Museum was established in 1960 by Key West native, Colonel Michell Wolfson, and his wife Frances. They saved and restored the historic building which had been the family home of Captain

John Geiger, Key West's first Harbor pilot. He had made his fortune as a wrecking master salvaging ships that foundered on the treacherous reefs.

This elegant 1846 example of American Classic Revival architecture is a perfect setting for the work of one of America's first truly original artists, John James Audubon, who visited the home while working on his famous bird images. The style of the house and Audubon's art represent the new flowering of American design that flourished in the early 19th century.

A wonderful tropical garden in the back is very enjoyable with collections of orchids, palm trees, and lilly pool.

Self guided audio tours daily. Their gallery of antique lithographs is across the street, and for collectors and admirers or Audubon's work, it is well worth a visit.

The End

www.ingramcontent.com/pod-product-compliance
Lightning Source LLC
Chambersburg PA
CBHW031058080526
44587CB00011B/730